'A wise, well-informed and clinically useful book that opens a way for mutual recognition and dialogue between Jungian analysis and relational psychoanalysis. Encouraging a turning away from the introversion so typical of the classical Jungian approach, there is also a possibility herein for further rapprochement between the descendants of Freud and those of Jung. This is going to be greatly facilitated by the emerging consensus that Jung may be considered a pioneer of relational psychoanalysis.'

Andrew Samuels, *Founder and board member of the International Association for Relational Psychoanalysis and Psychotherapy*

'The Relational Jung represents a carefully considered effort to free analytical psychology from its traditional intrapsychic bias to include interpersonal, synchronistic, and social dimensions of life. The essays are nuanced and form a bouquet of thoughtful contributions to this endeavor. It's a book to be recommended for teaching purposes in Jungian training programs.'

Murray Stein, PhD, *author of Outside, Inside and All Around*

The Relational Jung

Within this fascinating new volume, a group of prominent Jungian writers seek to explore the apparent contradiction between two aspects of Jungian thinking: one that points in the direction of a genuinely radical relational psychology, and another which seems to struggle to engage meaningfully with what we might call the psychosocial dimension.

Jung's work is centrally concerned with what is often referred to as the problem of opposites, for example, his notions of introversion and extraversion. In biographical terms, this is expressed in the split between Jung's outward-facing and inward-facing personalities. Because Jung identified himself as an introvert, the question arises as to how this might have shaped his psychology. Recent scholarship has often brought attention to the problematics of Jung's engagement with collective life and the political. In the spirit of maintaining the kind of dialectical tension that Jung urged, this series of papers seeks to explore one-sidedness in analytical psychology with particular emphasis on how we theorize the immediacy of encounter with others.

This unique collection will be of particular value to scholars and clinicians within the Jungian world, as well as relationally-oriented psychoanalysts with an interest in becoming more conversant in Jung.

Robin S. Brown, PhD, is a psychoanalyst in private practice who has served on faculty at Columbia University, Pacifica Graduate Institute, and the California Institute of Integral Studies. His first book, *Psychoanalysis Beyond the End of Metaphysics: Thinking Towards the Post-Relational* (Routledge, 2017), won the American Board and Academy of Psychoanalysis Book Prize. This was followed by *Groundwork for a Transpersonal Psychoanalysis: Spirituality, Relationship, and Participation* (Routledge, 2020).

Mark Saban, PhD, is a senior analyst with the Independent Group of Analytical Psychologists. He was until recently the Director of the MA in Jungian and Post-Jungian Studies at the University of Essex. His book, *'Two Souls Alas': Jung's Two Personalities and the Making of Analytical Psychology* (Chiron, 2019), won the International Association of Jungian Studies' Best Book of 2019.

The Relational Jung

Challenging the Inward Orientation of
Analytical Psychology

Edited by
Robin S. Brown and Mark Saban

Routledge
Taylor & Francis Group

LONDON AND NEW YORK

Designed cover image: The History Collection / Alamy Stock Photo

First published 2026
by Routledge
4 Park Square, Milton Park, Abingdon, Oxon OX14 4RN

and by Routledge
605 Third Avenue, New York, NY 10158

Routledge is an imprint of the Taylor & Francis Group, an informa business

British Library Cataloguing-in-Publication Data
A catalogue record for this book is available from the British Library

Library of Congress Cataloging-in-Publication Data
A catalog record has been requested for this book

ISBN: 978-1-032-55131-9 (hbk)
ISBN: 978-1-032-55130-2 (pbk)
ISBN: 978-1-003-42914-2 (ebk)

DOI: 10.4324/9781003429142

Typeset in Times New Roman
by Taylor & Francis Books

Contents

Figures

Contributors

Robin McCoy Brooks, MA, LMHC, TEP, is a Jungian analyst, international educator, and consultant in private practice in Seattle/Bellingham, WA, USA. She is the Co-Editor-in-Chief of the *International Journal of Jungian Studies* and serves on the Board of Directors of the International Association for Jungian Studies. Robin is an active analyst member of the Inter-Regional Society of Jungian Analysts and the International Association for Analytical Psychology, and a nationally certified Trainer, Educator and Practitioner of Group Psychotherapy, Sociometry and Psychodrama. She is the author of *Psychoanalysis Catastrophe & Social Action* (2022), which earned the title of "Best Applied Book 2022" from the International Association of Jungian Studies. Additionally, Robin has co-authored *The Healing Power of Community - Mutual Aid, AIDS, and Social Transformation in Psychology* (2024) with Lusijah Marx and Graham Harriman, in addition to numerous chapters and articles.

Robin S. Brown, PhD, LP, NCPsyA, is a psychoanalyst in private practice. He has served on faculty at Columbia University, Pacifica Graduate Institute, and the California Institute of Integral Studies. His first book, *Psychoanalysis Beyond the End of Metaphysics: Thinking Towards the Post-Relational*, won the American Board and Academy of Psychoanalysis Book Prize. This was followed by an edited collection, *Re-Encountering Jung: Analytical Psychology and Contemporary Psychoanalysis*, which was nominated for a Gradiva Award, and his second full-length work *Groundwork for a Transpersonal Psychoanalysis: Spirituality, Relationship, and Participation*. He is co-editor of *Emancipatory Perspectives on Madness: Psychological, Social, and Spiritual Dimensions*.

Joseph Cambray is a Jungian analyst, past President of the International Association of Analytical Psychology, and past President-CEO of Pacifica Graduate Institute. He has been a faculty member at the Harvard Medical School Center for Psychoanalytic Studies at Massachusetts General Hospital, Psychiatry Department. He is the former US Editor of the *Journal of Analytical Psychology*.

Warren Colman is a training and supervising analyst for the Society of Analytical Psychology and Consultant Editor of the *Journal of Analytical Psychology*. He teaches, lectures, and supervises internationally and has published many papers on diverse topics, including couple interaction, sexuality, the self, symbolic imagination, synchronicity, and the therapeutic process. He is the author of *Act and Image: The Emergence of Symbolic Imagination*, published in 2016.

Mark Saban, PhD, was until recently the director of the MA in Jungian and Post-Jungian Studies in the Department of Psychosocial and Psychoanalytic Studies, University of Essex. He trained with the Independent Group of Analytical Psychologists, with whom he is a senior analyst, working in Oxford. Publications: Mark co-edited (with Emilija Kiehl and Andrew Samuels) *Analysis and Activism - Social and Political Contributions of Jungian Psychology* (2016) and wrote *'Two Souls Alas': Jung's Two Personalities and the Making of Analytical Psychology* (2019) which won the International Association of Jungian Studies' Best Book of 2019.

Marcus West is a former Co-Editor-in-Chief of the *Journal of Analytical Psychology*. He is a Jungian therapist, a relational alchemist, and a soul journey companion. He is the author of three books, *Feeling, Being and the Sense of Self* (2007), *Understanding Dreams in Clinical Practice* (2011), and *Into the Darkest Places - Early Relational Trauma and Borderline States of Mind* (2016), as well as a number of papers, one of which was joint winner of the Michael Fordham Prize in 2004. He has taught widely in the UK and abroad.

Mark Winborn, PhD, NCPsyA, is a Jungian Psychoanalyst and Clinical Psychologist. He received his training in psychology from Michigan State University and the University of Memphis, and his analytic certificate from the Inter-Regional Society of Jungian Analysts. He is a training/supervising analyst of the I-RSJA and the C.G. Jung Institute in Zurich. His publications include *Deep Blues: Human Soundscapes for the Archetypal Journey* (2011), *Shared Realities: Participation Mystique and Beyond* (2014), *Interpretation in Jungian Analysis: Art and Technique* (2018), *Beyond Persona: On Individuation and Beginnings with Jungian Analysts* (2023), and *Jungian Psychoanalysis: A Contemporary Introduction* (2024).

Introduction

The challenge posed to any discourse that would seek to destabilize received norms is in having some practical influence on the status quo. Jung's concern for this question is one explanatory factor in considering the effort he exerted to frame his work as "scientific." In this way, Analytical Psychology was subject to many of the same foundational anxieties that shaped the work of Freud. At the turn of the 20th century, the intellectual climate of the fledgling field of psychology was informed by epistemological uncertainty. Central to this was a fear of contagion—the struggle to maintain a categorical difference between doctors and patients, and the related attempt to establish objectivity for the psychological standpoint. Yet any introspective psychology must forego the comfort of discretely observable behavior for a plane of observation that is more obviously subjective. While Jung characterized Freud's thinking as extroverted on the basis that Freud placed so much emphasis on sex, this claim is perhaps only valid in a relative sense. In practice, Freud's efforts to posit an experiential basis for psychological problems arose in opposition to the organic hypotheses of the time and in this context, it is surely Freud who stands as the defender of an introverted position in contrast to the more starkly extroverted sensibility of the Kraepelinian establishment.

Ironically, the role of "the relationship" in the work of Freud and Jung is minimized to a significant degree as a function of both figures' efforts to stay related to/accommodate the scientific milieu of the time. Both thinkers thus tended to forestall the more relational elements of their work in favor of a broader program wherein psyche is located "within" individuals more so than between them. In Freud this was perhaps expressed most obviously in the clinical approach he adopted—free association and the couch reflect an attempt to try to cordon off the patient's mind from that of the doctor.

The fate of this classical Freudian sensibility would depend on geographical context. Within the English-speaking world the development of Freud's work differs quite significantly on either side of the Atlantic. In the US, throughout much of the last century professional orthodoxy was closely guarded by means of the power wielded by the American Psychoanalytic Association and the New York Psychoanalytic. Significantly, being a medical doctor was long maintained as a prerequisite for acceptance into psychoanalytic training—a state of affairs that only changed following a lawsuit that was settled in 1989. In the UK, by contrast, the training of analysts from outside the medical profession has always been generally accepted. In North America, arguably the most significant line of thinking to emerge from the psychoanalytic milieu of the mid-20th century was reflected in the interpersonal tradition, yet the emergence of this tradition required that the William Alanson White Institute be founded as an independent entity in protest against the strictures of Freudian orthodoxy. The more ecumenical climate of the British Psychoanalytical Society was reflected in the "gentleman's agreement" reached in 1946 between Sylvia Payne, Anna Freud, and Melanie Klein. This agreement—leading to the institutionalization of the three groups (the Anna Freud group, the Middle group, and the Melanie Klein group)—demonstrates the relative flexibility of the British psychoanalytic establishment of the mid-20th century in accommodating new ideas.

The relational movement in American psychoanalysis started to emerge in the 1980s as a direct response to the restrictive intellectual climate that had dominated the profession for decades previously. Greenberg and Mitchell (1983) are often credited with launching the movement by seeking to draw parallels between developments in ego psychology, interpersonal thinking, self psychology, and British object relations theory. In the range of perspectives offered by these distinct schools, Greenberg and Mitchell recognized an overarching concern for the role of relationships in shaping who we are and how the psychotherapeutic process functions. Thus, the relational tradition began not on the strength of a uniquely original contribution to theory but more so as an effort to politically reconfigure the field. This endeavor coincided with the opening-up of the profession to psychologists and social workers, with the effect that many clinicians were now drawn to the field with quite different backgrounds and sensibilities than had been typical when psychoanalysis was treated as a medical specialty.

To a significant extent, the relational movement in psychoanalysis can be understood in terms of a rapprochement between practicing analysts and the academy. While Freudian psychoanalysis had always been transmitted via the hermeneutically-sealed environs of the independent institutes, it is apt that the relational tradition would find its spiritual home with the NYU post-doctoral training program. For decades Freudian orthodoxy had been significantly shielded from the wider intellectual climate by virtue of the ingrained power structures that had been established to protect it. To an extent, the shift in theoretical emphasis offered by the relational movement contrasts the climate of the US social sciences at the turn of the 21st century with the intellectual atmosphere of the medical field in Europe at the turn of the 20th.

As a distinctly American phenomenon, in its forcefulness and vitality the relational trend in psychoanalysis can be understood as a reaction to the restrictions previously imposed upon the field in the United States. The extensive body of ideas that would emerge from this political shift was thus occasioned in defiance of existing power structures. Such has been the success of this movement that relational thinking has grown over the last 40 years to become the new dominant power in American psychoanalysis.

The implications for Analytical Psychology in this turn of events are nuanced. For Jungians, the professional status of Jung's work and the sense of exclusion has tended to be understood in relationship to the idea of a restrictive Freudian orthodoxy. As previously touched upon, however, following Jung's lead this distinction has often been understood along typological lines. While Jung (1921) explicitly sought to position Analytical Psychology as an undertaking to reconcile the typological divide between what he considered the introverted stance of Alfred Adler and the extroverted psychology of Freud, this undertaking was contradicted to the extent that Jung also considered himself a defender of the introverted standpoint in contrast to the extroverted biases of Western civilization—as exemplified, according to Jung, by the materialist values of Freud's psychoanalysis. While relationalists have sought to revise Freud on the basis that he places too much emphasis on the individual, Jung's criticism tends in the opposite direction by critiquing Freud for insufficiently valuing interiority.

When it comes to Analytical Psychology's approach toward the relational, we find a set of problems that are interestingly different from those we find with psychoanalysis. The main difficulty is Jung's insistence upon taking up two contradictory positions.

On the one hand, when we look at those of Jung's writings that are devoted to the practice of psychotherapy (mostly to be found in Volume 16 of his *Collected Works* (Jung, 1975) and culminating in his "The Psychology of the Transference" (1946)) we are presented with a rich seam of proto-relational themes. In these texts, Jung prioritizes the mutuality of the analytic process:

> In any effective psychological treatment the doctor is bound to influence the patient; but this influence can only take place if the patient has a reciprocal influence on the doctor. You can exert no influence if you are not susceptible to influence.
>
> (Jung, 1929, §163)

For Jung, the analyst must and will always remain vulnerable to the impact of the patient:

> It is futile for the doctor to shield himself from the influence of the patient and to surround himself with a smoke-screen of fatherly and

professional authority. By so doing he only deprives himself of a highly important organ of information.

(Jung, 1929, §163)

In these texts, Jung seems not only to be differentiating Jungian analysis from the "blank screen" approach of classical psychoanalysis, but also, through the elaborate "alchemical" model of therapeutic work that he elaborates in "The Psychology of the Transference," to be seeking to develop, in a remarkably precise way, an approach to analytic work that can convey enormous relational complexity. Despite a persistent policy of deliberately eschewing the kind of detailed case studies which dominate psychoanalytic literature, Jung's alchemical articulation of therapeutic work nonetheless succeeds in communicating with great subtlety the numerous conscious and unconscious dynamic relational communications that can occur in either direction within the analytic field, and his description of the emergence of what he terms a "third" within that field is highly original (Jung, 1946, §399); a notion that has recently been re-invented (without mention of Jung) by various psychoanalytic writers (Benjamin, 2004; Ogden, 2004). It is these writings of Jung that have led several post-Jungians to describe him as a "pioneer of relational psychoanalysis" (Sedgwick, 2012; Samuels, 2012). Psychoanalyst Alberto Stefana even goes so far as to suggest that Jung was "the person who probably preceded everyone on the issue of countertransference" (Stefana, 2017, p. 35).

This is, however, far from being the whole picture. It also needs to be emphasized that the predominant focus of Jung's psychology (at least within the other 19 volumes of the *Collected Works*) is on the *individual psyche*, and this seems to result in an almost exclusive tendency to characterize the process of individuation as a thoroughly *intrapsychic* process which involves outer relationships only to the extent that they provide opportunities for projections that subsequently need to be withdrawn. This approach leads Jung in turn toward a model of analytic work that can only be described as "one-person." When Jung writes in this vein, we get the impression that the analyst's job is merely to provide the appropriate external, guiding, and educative environment within which the patient can follow their inner individuation journey. Moreover, this approach appears to have been characteristic of Jung's own clinical practice. Peter (Godwin) Baynes described his analysis with Jung in this way:

He is always in the background, felt rather than seen. He … seems to be hardly concerned with the actual nexus and incident of one's life. He is essentially a guide. He shows one the way but the actual business of analysis and self-evaluation he has left almost entirely to my own efforts. Actually, he knows very little about me and seems to care very little … yet I am as deeply under his directing influence as ever.

(Jansen, 2003, p. 129)

What we know of other patients' experiences of Jung seems to support this thoroughly unrelational picture (see Douglas, 1997, for a good example).

From Jung's own early experiences struggling with what he describes in *Memories, Dreams, Reflections* (1963) as his personality no. 2, through to the overwhelming emphasis upon interiority that characterizes his "confrontation with the unconscious" in *The Red Book*, along with his evident partiality for introversion as seen in his *Psychological Types* (Jung, 1921), there seems little doubt about the fact that Jung's "personal equation" exerted a distorting effect upon his psychology. Recent research by several post-Jungian writers has suggested that the influence of this factor upon the development of ana-lytical psychology has effectively endowed Jungian psychology with an ende-mic and persistent bias in the direction of the inner, the introverted, and the intrapsychic aspects of psyche. The consequence has been a persistent neglect of the outer, extraverted, and interpsychic dimensions of psychological life (Brown, 2014; Saban, 2019). Only some of this can be accounted for by what Jung undoubtedly saw as a pressing need to compensate for the one-sided extraversion of Western culture.

The overall effect of Jung's introverted bias, his tendency to highlight the archetypal, the alchemical, and the quasi-metaphysical (e.g. his research into synchronicity), and his reluctance to offer detailed clinical histories, has been that the radical and highly original focus on relation-ality to be found in his "The Psychology of the Transference"—a focus that points clearly in the direction of a *two-person* model of psychother-apy—has been more or less overlooked. It is hardly surprising to see that many of Jung's followers have subsequently neglected this whole dimension of Jung's thinking.[1]

During his life, Jung managed, by force of character, to maintain what seemed to be a coherent psychological approach—albeit one that contained numerous implicit contradictions. In the post-Jungian period, however, the theoretical unity of Jung's psychology has shown itself to be fragile and fissile. The history of Analytical Psychology since Jung's death is characterized by splits and schisms, whereby various factions have chosen to highlight certain favored aspects of the Jungian consensus while ignoring or rejecting others. If we employ the taxonomy of the post-Jungian field developed by Andrew Samuels (1985b), we can see how this has played out in the arena of the clinic. Analysts in the so-called Classical school have generally preferred to follow Jung's actual practice, predominantly working with the symbolic through dreams, myths, and fairy tales. This school has consequently paid relatively little attention to the relational (and transferential) complexities to be found in the consulting room. While we might have expected the Devel-opmental school, which has historically demonstrated a great interest in the clinical dimension and especially in the intricacies of transference and coun-tertransference, to have shown more interest in Jung's own idiosyncratic approach to the relational, what we often find instead is the incorporation of the ideas of Kleinian or Winnicottian object relations. By contrast, the third, Archetypal school, tends to exclusively focus upon the "soul" realm within which archetypal dynamics play out. Hillman and his followers have shown very little interest in what tends to be dismissed as the merely "personal." In the work of Wolfgang Giegerich, for example, an interest in the relational is characterized as insufficiently "soul"-oriented to even count as a psychological concern at all.

Perhaps this explains why, despite Jung's own theoretical exploration of relational themes, Jungian psychology has not undergone an explicitly relational revolution. However, the Jungian field has been significantly impacted in recent decades by the development of Jungian studies as a distinct academic discipline. Pacifica Graduate Institute on the West Coast of the US and the University of Essex in the UK are two of the more noteworthy institutions to attract large numbers of students with an interest in studying Analytical Psychology in a non-clinical academic context. Further supported by the emergence of the International Association for Jungian Studies, these developments have led to Jungian literature being more directly informed by broader trends within academia. Thus, the political and psychosocial emphasis in relational psychoanalysis, in so far as this emphasis reflects academic trends more broadly, has been paralleled with a similar tendency in Analytical Psychology. Jungian authors now routinely tackle subject matter reflecting an underlying concern with social context—politics, race, gender, and sexuality. While these themes have historically been neglected within the field, they are now mainstays of Jungian literature.

Less emphasized are considerations of the relational in the more immediate sense as expressed paradigmatically in terms of how we think about clinical work. While the relational turn in American psychoanalysis began with a focus on the clinical application of psychoanalytic theory and later developed more of a focus on broader sociocultural themes, the initial clinical emphasis of the relational movement doesn't have an obvious Jungian counterpart. Whilst the vast majority of relational psychoanalytic authors tend to be practicing clinicians coming from a culture that strongly values contextualizing theory in clinical practice, the quiet revolution in Jungian studies has sometimes been driven by scholars who are not themselves clinicians. Meanwhile, the clinical practice of Analytical Psychology has continued to develop largely in isolation from the psychoanalytic world. While references to relational psychoanalysis can be found in Jungian literature, they are patchy at best, and a substantial reckoning with the challenges of the relational movement has yet to be undertaken.

The editors of this book believe that this relative lack of engagement is a loss for both sides. If with the suggestive yet clinically-unformulated nature of "The Psychology of the Transference" Jung's psychology can be considered proto-relational, in a more challenging sense Jung's work may also be configured as post-relational (Brown, 2017, 2020). Whilst abandoning the "experience near" (Kohut, 1977) emphasis that the relational enterprise tends to favor, the abstractions of Jung's metapsychology nevertheless may offer a theoretical footing notably absent from the relational literature—this being reflected most obviously in his foundational emphasis on the *collectivity* of the unconscious.[2] Conversely, Jung's psychology also enables us to understand the relational sensibility as being reflective of a particular typological and/or archetypal lens, thus perhaps moderating or nuancing the claims of this position. His work may therefore be configured as post-relational both in offering a metapsychology that is more fully relational in its own right and in the ways that this metapsychology seeks to situate the relational in tension with a psychology of individuation. Fleshing out these ideas in greater detail is beyond the scope of the present introduction, but the reciprocal possibilities we see in a further exchange between schools are extensive.

Notes

1 Notable exceptions are: Jacoby (1984), Sedgwick (1994, 2012), Schwartz-Salant (1995, 1998) Field (1991), and Samuels (1985, 2012).
2 As one of us has argued previously (Brown, 2016, 2017), in the absence of such a foundation relational writers often come to lean on positivistic assumption in such a way that their underlying supports might be argued inherently non-relational.

References

Benjamin, J. (2004). Beyond doer and done to: An intersubjective view of thirdness. *Psychoanalytic Quarterly*, 73, 5–46.

Brown, R.S. (2014). Evolving attitudes. *International Journal of Jungian Studies*, 6(3), 243–253.

Brown, R.S. (2017). *Psychoanalysis Beyond the End of Metaphysics: Thinking Towards the Post-Relational*. Routledge.

Brown, R.S. (2018). Where do minds meet? Intersubjectivity in light of Jung, In R.S. Brown (Ed.), *Re-Encountering Jung: Analytical Psychology and Contemporary Psychoanalysis*. Routledge.

Brown, R.S. (2020). *Groundwork for a Transpersonal Psychoanalysis: Spirituality, Relationship, and Participation*. Routledge.

Douglas, C. (1997). *Translate This Darkness: The Life of Christiana Morgan, the Veiled Woman in Jung's Circle*. Princeton University Press.

Field, N. (1991). Projective identification: Mechanism or mystery? *The Journal of Analytical Psychology*, 36(1), 93–109.

Greenberg, J.R., and Mitchell, S.A. (1983). *Object Relations in Psychoanalytic Theory*. Harvard University Press.

Jacoby, M. (1984). *The Analytic Encounter: Transference and Human Relationship*. Inner City Books.

Jansen, D.B. (2003). *Jung's Apprentice: A Biography of Helton Godwin Baynes*. Daimon Verlag.

Jung, C.G. (1921). Psychological types. In C.J. Jung, *Collected Works, Vol*. 6. Princeton University Press.

Jung, C.G. (1929). Problems of modern psychotherapy. In C.J. Jung, *Collected Works, Vol*. 16 (paras. 114–174). Princeton University Press.

Jung, C.G. (1946). The psychology of the transference. In C.J. Jung, *Collected Works, Vol*. 16 (paras. 353–539). Princeton University Press.

Jung, C.G. (1963). *Memories, Dreams, Reflections* (R. Winston & C. Winston, Trans.; A. Jaffe, Ed.). Pantheon Books.

Jung, C.G. (1975). *Collected Works, Vol*. 16: *Practice of Psychotherapy: Essays on the Psychology of the Transference and other subjects*, 2nd Ed. Princeton University Press.

Kohut H. (1977). *The Restoration of the Self*. International Universities Press.

Ogden, T.H. (2004). The analytic third: Implications for psychoanalytic theory and technique. *Psychoanalytic Quarterly*, 73, 167–195.

Saban, M. (2019) *'Two Souls Alas': Jung's Two Personalities and the Making of Analytical Psychology*. Chiron Press.

Samuels, A. (1985a). Countertransference, the "mundus imaginalis" and a research project. *The Journal of Analytical Psychology*, 30(1), 47–71.

Samuels, A. (1985b). *Jung and the Post-Jungians*. Routledge.

Samuels, A. (2012) "The analyst is as much 'in the analysis' as the patient" (1929): Jung as a pioneer of relational psychoanalysis. Unpublished paper delivered at 10th Anniversary Conference of the International Association for Relational Psychotherapy and Psychoanalysis, New York, March 1–4, 2012.

Schwartz-Salant, N. (1995) On the interactive field as an analytic object. In M. Stein (Ed.), *The Interactive Field in Analysis* (pp. 1–36). Chiron Press

Schwartz-Salant, N. (1998) *The Mystery of Human Relationship*. Routledge.

Sedgwick, D. (1994). *The Wounded Healer: Counter-Transference from a Jungian Perspective*. Routledge.

Sedgwick, D. (2012). Jung as a pioneer of relational analysis. Unpublished paper delivered at 10th Anniversary Conference of the International Association for Relational Psychotherapy and Psychoanalysis, New York, March 1–4, 2012.

Stefana, A. (2017). *History of Countertransference: From Freud to the British Object Relations School*. Routledge.

Chapter 1

Jung and the Relational

Beyond the Individual

Mark Saban

Introduction

Jung is of course the writer of the archetype. However, it is also true to say that his writings tend to concentrate upon the ways in which archetypes show up *within* the individual psyche. Where Jungians and post-Jungians have applied these ideas of Jung to the analytic process, they have mostly paid attention to how the archetype shows up in intrapsychic dynamics. What concerns them are the ways in which the archetype furthers individuation as an individual, inner process. Since, however, Jung posits the archetype as a *collective* phenomenon, it seems valid to explore the ways in which analysis as a relational phenomenon transcends the individuality of either of its participants.

The relational is usually characterized as something that constellates an interpersonal bond or nexus between already-constituted individuals. Such an approach inevitably puts the psychological focus firmly upon the individual psyche, and particularly on the way these relational bonds are experienced as contributing to the intrapsychic development or individuation of the individual. Relatively little attention has been paid to the nature and importance of this relational bond *in itself* —considered as an archetypal factor that transcends the inner processes of the individuals involved.

By sticking closely to this phenomenon of relationality, I hope to shake free of the narrow focus—often found in classical Jungian writings—upon psychological processes *as they are experienced within individuals*. By looking beyond the limits of the atomized individual, I am therefore attempting to adumbrate a conception of the relational that can properly support and further what I understand to be the implicitly *radical* implications of Jung's psychology. This project necessarily requires the very notion of the individual itself to be put into question. However, although such an approach inevitably challenges the usual assumptions of analytical psychology, it is Jung's own emphasis—in various contexts—upon the essentially *collective* nature of the psyche (not to mention the theoretical direction of his later psychology) that provides me with both the theoretical background and the teleological thrust required.

DOI: 10.4324/9781003429142-1

In short, my aim is to focus upon the individuation of *the analytic process itself* by exploring the ways in which the archetypal and/or the collective unconscious manifest within and through specifically *relational* dynamics.

Jung and Others on the Intersubjective

As Robin Brown has described with admirable clarity, the relational school of psychoanalysis has developed a bundle of notions that we might broadly describe as intersubjective (Brown, 2017). These revolve around what Aron (1996) has called a "meeting of minds," Benjamin (1999) a "mutual recognition," and Ogden (2004) and Benjamin (2004) (in differing ways) "the third." Although there are important differences between these ideas, they do all seek to explore a kind of relationality that challenges and undermines conventional psychoanalytic ideas about the individual, the intrapsychic, and one-person analysis. This notion of intersubjectivity has therefore challenged the narrow concept of relationship we find not only in classical psychoanalysis but also in object relations. Nonetheless, because, as Brown points out, these ideas seem to lack a coherent explanatory background or metaphysical grounding, they display a persistent tendency to revert to Cartesian modes of thinking and thereby lose touch with the more radical potential of what we might call a more fully relational approach.

Like other post-Jungians (Samuels, 2012; Colman, 2013; Sedgwick, 2026), Brown is interested in possible overlaps between psychoanalytic and Jungian approaches to the deep-relational in analysis. His conclusion is that the emerging notion of intersubjectivity in the psychoanalytic tradition "might benefit from a more direct engagement with Jung" (Brown, 2017, p. 179), precisely because Jung offers the theoretical grounding that tends to be lacking in the literature of relational psychoanalysis.

In Jung's psychology (and especially his late psychology of synchronicity and the *Unus Mundus*), self and other are regarded as different aspects of a transcendent unity. Although Jung's writings on this topic can sometimes seem problematically abstract or esoteric, his theoretical insights do possess the capacity to bear usefully upon the deep-relational phenomena that he observes and analyses in his "The Psychology of the Transference" (Jung, 1946). Unfortunately, as Sedgwick has pointed out (Sedgwick, 1994, p. 5), Jung's general reluctance in his published writings to offer detailed clinical examples makes it difficult to identify specific interlacings between the archetypal, the synchronistic, and the countertransferential as they operate within the analytic container. We can nonetheless infer from various alchemical hints that Jung understands the shared (and perhaps transpersonal) quality of the analytic encounter to be intimately entwined with the archetypal realm, and that it is precisely this dimension that manifests as "the third."

Transindividuation in Analysis

In an attempt to locate an experiential ground for a discussion that can easily start to feel highly theoretical, I therefore intend to concentrate here upon the analytic encounter, and specifically the way in which its various lines of relation both reflect and express a collective dimension of psyche. What I have found useful here is Gilbert Simondon's notion of "transindividuation" (Simondon, 2020; Combes, 2013).[1] With the *transindividual*, Simondon provides a philosophically coherent notion of "the third" as an energetic field of the psycho-social collective that lies outside and prior to any links or connections between individual subjects. As I will attempt to show, Simondon's rigorous focus on the *transindividual* dimension of individuation brings into focus those collective aspects of the analytic process that transcend both intrapsychic dynamics and interpersonal dynamics. By incorporating some of Simondon's insights, we can begin to provide some rigor to the Jungian approach, and thus more effectively challenge those residual post-Cartesian assumptions which, as we have seen, still linger in many psychoanalytic understandings of the relational.

Jung's late psychology focuses on the creative encounter between inner and outer dimensions of psychological life. The writings on synchronicity, the *Unus Mundus*, the psychoid, alchemy, and transference/countertransference, in varying ways take on the task of tackling this inner/outer problem. Jung points to the importance of this conceptual shift in *Memories, Dreams, Reflections*. At the time of his confrontation with the unconscious, he says, he "felt the gulf between the external world and the interior world of images in its most painful form," seeing "only an irreconcilable contradiction between 'inner' and 'outer'" (Jung & Jaffé, 1989, p. 194). As he explains, what is clear to him *now* (i.e. at the end of his life) is what he calls the "interaction of both worlds." This late recognition of the dynamic interplay between the inner and outer has enormous implications for Jung's attitude to the relational.

In "The Psychology of the Transference" Jung clearly states that individuation requires that both the intrapsychic and the interpersonal dimensions of individuation possess equal emphasis and, moreover, that they are intimately interrelated:

> Individuation has two principal aspects: in the first place it is an internal and subjective process of integration, and in the second it is an equally indispensable process of objective relationship. Neither can exist without the other, although sometimes the one and sometimes the other predominates.
> (Jung, 1946, §448)

Jung gives as much weight to the outer-relational dimension as he does to the intrapsychic. The process of individuation (undergone via repeated operations of the process he describes as the transcendent function) requires not only a constant ongoing relational encounter with *inner* others (in the form of complexes, archetypes, etc.), but also an encounter with *outer* others.

In the subsequent paragraph Jung points up the relevance of this point to the analytic process itself and makes a crucial clarification: what occurs in analysis transcends the individuation of any single person. Indeed, Jung goes much further; he insists that it also has a wider psycho-social relevance: "[T]he bond established by the transference—however hard to bear and however incomprehensible it may seem—is vitally important not only for the individual but also for society" (Jung, 1946, §449). Jung's implication is that because the transferential/countertransferential process offers a concentratedly dynamic example of the interplay between inner and outer, it is precisely here that the relationship between the personal and the societal is most richly played out.

At first glance, such a claim seems at best overblown. Indeed, the post-Jungian Wolfgang Giegerich expresses just such reservations. Giegerich (2010, p. 251) objects to what he sees as grotesquely inflated claims for "the therapist's work in the consulting room," arguing that Jung is making a kind of category error, illegitimately mixing up two different dimensions of the opus: a) the ordinary personal, and b) the "fundamental truths, the open questions and deep conflicts of the age." In fact, for Giegerich, Jung is making a threefold mistake. First, he is illegitimately prioritizing the inner aspect of the individual. Second, he is wrongly understanding "mankind's problems" to be atemporal and archetypal. Third, he is failing to recognise that "the small dreams of the ordinary individual are only of private, personal significance" (Giegerich, 2010, p. 254).

All of these allegations possess some cogency with regard to Jung's work in general. However, with regard to the specific argument that Jung is making here, Giegerich has surely missed the point. Firstly, Jung goes out of his way to emphasize that it is *not* the solely inner aspect of psychological work that is critical here but rather the *interplay* between inner and outer as it manifests in the microcosm of the analytic vessel. Secondly, this interplay itself entails, for Jung, a meeting between the present/historical and the unchanging/timeless.

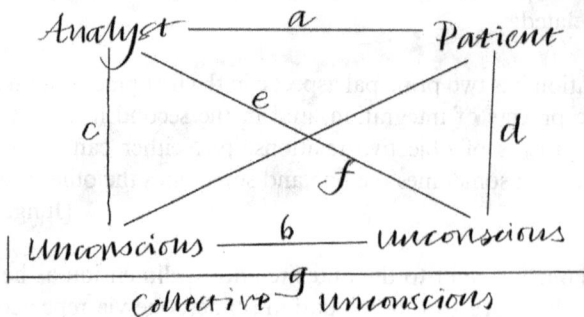

Figure 1.1

Finally, Jung is clearly arguing that any meaning that emerges out of the dynamic interaction between intrapsychic and interpersonal (as it unfolds through the analytic relationship) should be seen as possessing particular interest precisely because it succeeds in bringing both the local and the collective into play.

Relational Vectors in Analysis

One way to think about these claims of Jung is to focus on the uniquely potent combination of relational vectors he identifies within the analytic event. We can differentiate some of these vectors by using Jung's helpful diagram (see fig. 1.1. which takes a form that is slightly different from what we see in "The Psychology of the Transference" (1946, §422)).[2]

Line "a" represents relations between the two constituted individuals operating on a conscious and conventional level (i.e. ordinary interpersonal relations). Lines "c" and "d" represent relations between the ego and the unconscious of each individual (i.e. intrapsychic relations). Lines "e" and "f" represent relations between the conscious ego of each individual and the unconscious of the other (i.e. unconscious projections—transferences—operating between the two participants). Line "b" represents unconscious relations between the two partners. This latter relational vector is, for obvious reasons, the hardest to bring to awareness and its dynamics are therefore easily missed. The whole complex of dynamics is in a sense contained within "g"—the collective unconscious.

It is important to be aware that all psychological diagrams have severe limitations. It is, for example, entirely artificial to understand Jung's lines and levels of relation as discretely differentiated; not only because they are all active at the same time (even if from one moment to the other one vector of relationality may be dominant and the others less so), but also because all lines of relation frequently resonate with other lines, thus engendering bewildering levels of complexity. This is why Jung describes the meeting of these vectors of relationality by evoking a "chemical" bond or combination: "When two chemical substances combine, both are altered. This is precisely what happens in the transference" (1946, §358).

For the purposes of this chapter, we need to focus on the way this bond brings together three dimensions: a) the intrapsychic, b) the inter-personal, and c) a "third" emergent field that transcends a and b. It is this combination that enables Jung to suggest that individuation is not only "an internal and subjective process of integration" but also an "indispensable process of objective relationship" (Jung, 1946, §448). Significant here is Jung's refusal to be satisfied with the idea that individuation is a narrowly personal and individual process and his consequent insistence that the psychosocial dimension of transference is "vitally important not only for the individual but also for society" (Jung, 1946, §448).

Synchronicity

Jung's new way of understanding the interplay between inner and outer can also be identified in his notion of synchronicity. As Cambray has noted, Jungians tend to discuss synchronicity in two quite different ways: either as "evidence of archetypal processes at work" (2004, p. 234) or alternatively as a "commentary on the state of the transference/countertransference relationship" (2004, p. 235). Cambray astutely points out that this dichotomy mirrors a fissure in the post-Jungian tradition between a "classical" approach that focuses primarily upon the symbolic/archetypal and a "developmental" approach that focuses on clinical dynamics, and especially transference/countertransference. I have elsewhere drawn attention to the ways in which Jung's own personality and, by extension, his psychology, seem to be at their most creative when they sit in the difficult tension between conflicting positions (Saban, 2019). Here too, then, the point of most interest seems to me to reside not in either of these two ways to view synchronicity but rather in the tension between them. This requires us to maintain a focus on the interplay between the archetypal dimension and the transference/countertransference dimension of the synchronistic event.

With this in mind, let us start with the example Jung most often uses to illustrate synchronicity: the incident of the scarab beetle (Jung, 1952, §843ff). As is often the case, Jung tells us very little about the clinical history that has led up to this moment. However, we now know that the patient mentioned in the story of the scarab synchronicity was Madeleine Reichstein Quarles van Ufford (1894–1975) who analysed with Jung probably between 1919 and 1924 (de Moura, 2014). Interestingly, she was also the patient who constellated a well-known dream of Jung's, which he recounts in *Memories, Dreams, Reflections* as an example of psychic compensation. This was the dream he referred to when he explained (in about 1930) to Peter Baynes that he had once been

> caught by a counter-transference to a beautiful aristocratic girl [Reichstein] and how he had a dream in which she was enthroned very high on an Eastern temple, high above him. And this explained how all his knowledge and interest in Oriental ideas and feelings had developed out of his transference to the girl. He had, as he said, to cut off his head and learn to submit his ignorance to his patient.
>
> (Jansen, 2003, pp. 244–5)

This information about (a) Jung's personal involvement with (and anima projection onto) Reichstein and b) the ways this played into certain theoretical developments in analytical psychology can now be incorporated into our wider understanding of the nature of the analytic/relational field at the time of the scarab synchronicity.

In his own account Jung is careful to narrowly limit the psychological information he offers by focusing upon the pathological state of Reichstein as an individual. She is, he tells us, animus-possessed and armored by an impenetrable Cartesian rationalism. However, taking into account what we now know, and reviewing the whole situation in terms of the vectored diagram in Figure 1.1, what emerges is a strikingly high level of relational complexity (in the form, for example, of anima/animus projections and counter-projections). This complexity is entirely relevant to the sticky relational bind that both participants apparently experienced. As Jung puts it, "the treatment had got stuck and there seemed to be no way out of the impasse" (Jung, 1952, §847). What Jung is describing is an impasse *of the whole field* not merely one occurring within either patient or analyst as separate individuals.

This matters because it was this blockage (with all its chaotic affective energy) that constellated the synchronicity. Reichstein attends a session in which she recounts a dream of being "given a golden scarab" (Jung, 1952, §843). At this point Jung, hearing something at the window, opens it, and in flies a "scarabaeid beetle" which Jung catches and hands to the patient with the words, "Here is your scarab" (Jung, 1952, §982).

In Jung's rather one-sided account of the event, we are told that the arrival of the beetle had the effect of enabling the patient's "natural being" to "burst through the armour of her animus possession", and that this (intrapsychic) breakthrough meant that "the process of transformation could at last begin to move" (Jung, 1952, §845). Significantly, he makes no comment on his own process or indeed on the analytic field as a whole. What he wants us to understand is that it is the patient's intrapsychic problem that has hitherto blocked her personal individuation, and that the synchronistic phenomenon has now succeeded in unblocking it.

However, by highlighting instead the *relational* impasse in the field between analyst and analysand, and by putting to one side the individuation of the patient (or indeed of Jung), we can now concentrate upon *the individuation of the interactive relational field* within which the analysis occurred.

Strictly speaking, it is the patient's dream that initiates the synchronicity. In 1934 Jung wrote to James Kirsch: "In the deepest sense, we all dream not out of ourselves but out of what lies between us and the other" (Jung, 1973, p. 172). In other words, the dream, because it is an archetypal event, does not belong solely to the dreamer and nor does it necessarily communicate only to the dreamer. Dreams—and synchronicities—are both constellated by and addressed to the analytic field itself as a transcendent third. In this case then, it seems likely that the dream is pointing directly to "what lies between" Jung and Reichstein.

Furthermore, as Roderick Main has shown, the image of the scarab was powerfully numinous *for Jung* long before this particular scarab flew into the consulting room (Main, 2013). A scarab featured in the vision that began Jung's 1913 confrontation with the unconscious (Jung, 1989, p. 179), and its mythic/symbolic significance was explored in *The Red Book* (Jung, 2009, p.

271). As Main has carefully traced, Jung was also well acquainted with the scarab's alchemical significance (Main, 2013, pp. 140ff). In brief, the appearance of the scarab at this moment—a scarab that had in the past appeared to Jung precisely when he had himself been experiencing states of inner impasse—would have inevitably evoked for him powerful archetypal motifs of death and rebirth. As we have seen, Jung told Baynes that with Reichstein he had had to "cut off his head and learn to submit his ignorance to his patient." This image itself resonates with Jung's 1913 vision in which the appearance of the scarab immediately follows the image of the dead hero with blood gushing from his head (Jung & Jaffé, 1989, p. 179). In both cases, the appearance of the scarab marked a painful realization that what was required was the death of the heroic thinking ego. As Main puts it, the "incident involving the scarab beetle was a synchronicity not only for the patient but also for Jung" (Main, 2013, p. 137). In light of all this, Jung's insistence that the problem was the *patient's* psychological inaccessibility and "intellectual resistance" (Jung, 1952, §982) begins to sound suspiciously like projection.

However, if we wish to move beyond individual pathology, we might find it more fruitful to focus instead upon the resonance between Reichstein's block and Jung's block, and indeed the resonance between Reichstein's scarab and Jung's scarab. Such an approach might also help explain Jung's "irritation with [Reichstein's] rationalism" and the "barely concealed pleasure he took in offering up the synchronistic beetle with a flourish" (Cambray, 2004, p. 236). For Jung, as Cambray puts it, "the image [of the scarab] evoked a time of great suffering, both personal and collective, that could not be relieved by rational understanding" (Cambray, 2004, p. 236).

It seems then that the changes brought about by the synchronistic appearance of the beetle showed up in three discernible arenas. First, as Jung tells us, the patient achieved an inner breakthrough; the "Cartesian rationalism" which armored her against her own unconscious could now be dismantled. Second, if Main and Cambray are correct, it was the appearance of the scarab, evoking previous moments in which Jung had achieved individuational breakthroughs (and particularly when he was required to "cut off his head") that awakened Jung to his capacity to move beyond his own fixed positions and enter the relational dimension of the analysis. However, alongside these two primarily *intrapsychic* shifts, it is important to note a third transformational dimension, within which the synchronistic scarab-event enabled both parties to become aware of and enter into a relational interactive field *that transcended both of them as separate individuals*. What had been hitherto experienced by both participants as a state of mutual frustration and impasse could only now shift into a phase in which "treatment could … be continued with satisfactory results" (Jung, 1952, §982). This is a field that could actively transcend the rational Cartesian perspective that keeps subject (analyst) discretely separate from object (patient), inner separate from outer. Clinically, what this means is that although individual breakthroughs are experienced within each participant, a simultaneous collective breakthrough also emerges on a third transindividual level.

From a relational point of view, the scarab-event (by which I mean the whole phenomenon, incorporating the patient's dream, the beetle's appearance at the window, and Jung's triumphant "Here is your scarab") attains its transmutational potential by simultaneously operating on *all* the vectors in Jung's diagram—intrapsychic, interpersonal and transindividual.

The synchronicity brings into relief the ways in which participants in analysis are linked in the deep unconscious. This takes us beyond individuality as atomised state of separateness. Cambray suggests that the "third" here represents the combination of *all* the relational vectors in Jung's diagram and is therefore "co-constructed from our mutual experiences, conscious and unconscious, atop an archetypal base" (Cambray, 2012, p. 85). In order to begin to understand the complexity of the clinical situation, then, we need to enable the use of *all* these vectors as different lenses through which to view it. When they come into play together, the multi-dimensional image that emerges is more than the sum of its parts. By understanding the transindividual in these terms, we can begin to transcend the narrowness and poverty of conventional ideas of transference/countertransference.

In sum, a synchronicity within the analytic frame of the kind Jung describes succeeds in working on several levels at once. Though it conveys a powerful sense of affectivity, experienced on the personal level as emotion, its archetypal nature takes it far beyond the experience of narrow subjectivity by initiating the participants into a shared, collective zone. Such an event remains highly relational in that it expresses and furthers intimate and profound links between the analyst and analysand. However, none of those links can be reduced to the merely personal/individual.

Affect and the Transindividual

Jung chooses to specifically highlight the emotional aspect of the archetypal experience: archetypes, he tells us, "are images *and at the same time emotions. One can speak of an archetype only when these two aspects coincide*" (Jung, 1961, §589, my italics). When Jung tries to express what if feels like for a subject to experience the archetypal, he often uses the word "numinous", by which he seems to mean "an affective, living experience that overflows the boundaries of the ego" (Huskinson, 2006, p. 200). The value of the numinous for Jung resides in the fact that it simultaneously highlights two different dimensions of the experience: the affective and the transpersonal. Our conventional ways of talking about emotions (and I include both psychoanalytic and Jungian approaches) habitually locate them *within* the subject. However, with numinosity we encounter an affect that is experienced by the subject not as a personal individual experience but as somehow emanating from the other (whether it be

God, nature, or the sublime). In effect, when Jung invokes the numinous, he is pointing to an affective experience that is bigger than any individual:

> Whenever ... in an excess of affect, in an emotionally excessive situation, I come up against a paradoxical fact or happening, I am in the last resort encountering an aspect of God, which I cannot judge logically and cannot conquer because it is stronger than me—because, in other words, it has a numinous quality ... I cannot "conquer" a numinosum, I can only open myself to it, let myself be overpowered by it, trusting in its meaning.
>
> (Jung, 1959, §864)

Jung's emphasis upon the collective aspect of affect becomes greatly clarified and expanded in Simondon. Simondon highlights the specifically *relational* role of affect in transindividual processes. We can also find useful discussions about precisely this topic in the literature of the so-called "affective turn" (Clough, 2007), a fertile interdisciplinary development that has taken place within the fields of human geography, philosophy, psychology, sociology, and body studies, and which finds a line of descent through Spinoza and Deleuze.

Spinoza describes affect simply as the capacity to affect and to be affected (Massumi, 2015, p. ix). When we affect or are affected by other people, or other things, we are *in relationship* with the other, whether the experience shows up on the inner or the outer plane. In other words, affect puts me in touch with and highlights wider relational processes. As Brian Massumi puts it, affects are "our angle of participation in processes larger than ourselves. With intensified affect comes a stronger sense of embeddedness in a larger field of life—a heightened sense of belonging, with other people and to other places." (Massumi, 2015, p. 6) This notion that affect is primarily relational has been noted elsewhere. Burkitt, for example, suggests that,

> if emotions are expressive of anything it is the relations and inter-dependencies of which they are an integral part, and in this sense emotions are essentially communicative – they are expressions occurring *between people* and not expressions of something contained inside a single person.
>
> (Burkitt, 1997, p. 40)

The transformative aspect of affect thus stems from its capacity to initiate us into a world of relationality that transcends our individual ego-emotions and ego-thoughts. Undoubtedly, in its intensity, affect is felt personally and subjectively. Nonetheless, this doesn't obviate its capacity to simultaneously put us in touch with a non-personal, non-subjective, non-individual dimension of life. As we become aware of the collective nature of affect, what changes for us is not our specific emotional response (which continues to be felt on the personal level) but our felt understanding of what it means in terms of our connection to the world.

Affect in the Consulting Room

It is this transindividual dimension of affect that shows up very clearly in the clinical writings of post-Jungian analyst and writer, Nathan Schwartz-Salant. Building on Jung's ideas on the role of the "third" in analysis, Schwartz-Salant developed the notion of the "interactive field" (Schwartz-Salant, 1988). What is useful about this thinking is that it prioritizes the field over the individual subjects who occupy it. Schwartz-Salant makes it clear that the field shows up particularly clearly through *affect*:

> [O]ne never knows if an affect of fear, anger, hate or love comes from the analysand or from the analyst ... [S]uch emotions exist as a quality of the interactive field ... a state in which the question of "whose contents" are being experienced cannot be determined.
>
> (Schwartz-Salant, 1998, p. 24).

In syzygy with this affective dimension, Schwartz-Salant also emphasises the highly *relational* aspect of this field: it is, he says "a realm in which relations per se are the main object, rather than the things related, such as complexes belonging to one or the other person" (Schwartz-Salant, 1988, p. 50). The field Schwartz-Salant is naming here is precisely the archetypal/collective realm of relations that I am focusing on in this chapter.

For example, aware that a 50-year-old male patient's rage seems to be having a destructive effect on their work together, Schwartz-Salant asks his patient "if anger [is] attacking the connection between us," and the patient responds by asking: "Whose anger?" At this point, Schwartz-Salant admits to the patient that there is "no way to know." All that could be known, he remarks, was that "we were both in a kind of energy field in which anger was present." Both partners thus entertained the possibility that the rage was a quality of "the field" rather than an emotion that "belonged" to either partner, and this brought about "a change in the quality of awareness of the texture and space around us" (Schwartz-Salant, 1988, pp. 89–90). Both participants now felt, Schwartz-Salant says, "as if an 'other' was present with us" (Schwartz-Salant, 1988, p. 90).

At times, this took the form of the participants feeling "inside and contained by" the field but at other times it was experienced as something "in the space between [them]" (Schwartz-Salant, 1988, p. 90). They were somehow both the "subject" of the field while also its "object." In effect, both participants were simultaneously contained in, connected between, and confronted by an affective phenomenon whose autonomy was experienced as something neither intrapsychic nor interpersonal, inner or outer.

Schwartz-Salant points out that when a field of this kind is constellated there is a strong temptation for the analyst to "sidestep ... the encounter" (Schwartz-Salant, 1988, p. 90). Such an avoidance might show up in the form of a reductive transference/countertransference interpretation. One might, for example highlight one's own feelings of abandonment in the face of the patient's fragmentation or attribute the patient's fear to his childhood relationship with his father. For all their plausibility, interpretations of this kind have the capacity to reductively undermine the transformative potential of a shared affective event. They are, in Schwartz-Salant's words, "too limited and repressive of the field between [analyst and patient]" (Schwartz-Salant, 1988, p. 87).

A Jungian analyst might be faced with a further temptation: to introduce an *archetypal* amplification. For example, she might suggest (like Schwartz-Salant at an earlier point in the same analysis), that what is going on is to do with the myth of the son/lover (Schwartz-Salant, 1998, p. 87). Though such an interpretation seems on the face of it to honor the *collective* nature of the phenomenon, it can however be highly destructive. First, it tends to bolster the analyst's own authority (qua *expert*) and thus breaks down the mutuality of the shared experience of affect. Second, by reframing the experience into what is primarily an intellectual/aesthetic form, it diverts attention from the essentially *affective* quality of the shared experience. In such cases, as Schwartz-Salant notes, although both partners consciously feel "more in control and far less fragmented ... the experience between [them becomes] soulless, and embodiment in any depth [is] not possible." (Schwartz-Salant, 1998, p. 88) It would seem that we need to distinguish an intervention that invokes an archetype from a genuinely archetypal engagement. Only the latter initiates both parties into the collective field of affect.

To continue Schwartz-Salant's account, once the affect is tolerated "without [either participant] knowing whose it was," what then occurs is that both analyst and patient begin to "feel an energized sense of ... body and its aliveness [becoming] conscious of our bodies as energy fields" (Schwartz-Salant, 1998, p. 90). A change in the nature of the field manifests: "[The patient] felt that his body wanted to embrace mine, and I could also feel this sense of embrace, indeed, of a longing for him." As Schwartz-Salant puts it, the *coniunctio* now manifests in the form of "a pair of opposites defining our interactional space: rage and longing" (Schwartz-Salant, 1998, p. 90). This means that both analyst and patient are held within a polar field movement (the alchemical field of *solve et coagula*) that transcends their separate individual emotional processes. It is now possible for the field to begin to work on the participants, rather than the participants working on the field. The polarity is not operating *between* the two individuals; it contains them and thus relieves both analyst and patient of the requirement to fall into polarized roles (for example, healthy/sick or healer/wounded, person-who-knows/person-who-learns). Schwartz-Salant points out that when a shared field of this kind is tolerated within analysis it can begin to transform not only the clinical field but also relationships that exist *outside* the field. In this case, we are told, for example, that the patient's relationship with his partner was now able to move beyond a hitherto intractable "incestuous pattern of destructive passion" (Schwartz-Salant, 1998, p. 91).

The Transindividuational Field

As we have seen, a field of this kind possesses a highly affective character. Its mutuality and intensity also create a sense of intimate relationality. The field possesses two contrasting aspects, two lenses through which it can be viewed. Through one lens each participant's experience can be regarded as highly personal and individual. To the extent that there are relations between participants they are inter-individual relations—individual to individual. However, through the other lens we see a different (transindividual) relation which possesses both archetypal and collective aspects. When both lenses are brought together into binocularity an entirely new perspective emerges which succeeds in binding together both the personal/individual and the collective. Just as 3D vision emerges out of the meeting of the individual 2D perspectives of each separate eye, and just as stereo audio emerges out of two different single monophonic sources, so does the transindividual enable a transformative shift to a relational perspective that cannot be retrospectively reduced to any single line of relation. It thus combines and retains *all* the relational vectors in Jung's diagram (Figure 1.1): a) conscious (ego) relations, b) intrapsychic relations, and c) those relational vectors (both individual projective and collective archetypal) that operate on the unconscious level. In effect, the individual qua individual is not erased but relativized, subsumed into a relational field which is experienced as transcending the personal/individualizing level of relation. Crucially, the individual level is not obliterated; instead it is maintained within the overall process, although in a new form.

The transindividuational phenomenon can thus be differentiated from the experience of participation mystique, which consists of a regressive possession by the group or mass, or a merger of the participants into total symbiosis. In a clinical event of transindividuation, the transformative dimension of the field is experienced as contributing to the individual/personal process of either or both of the participants. For example, in the scarab synchronicity, both Reichstein and Jung evidently come away from the experience with an increase in personal self-knowledge. However, beyond that there is also a wider (third) transformation of perspective which, in a sense, contains and subsumes this narrow aspect of personal development. The field that contains both Jung and Reichstein (and the scarab) is *itself* transformed in such a way that a third level of understanding is gained by the participants. This process cannot be observed through a lens that remains on the personal/individual level. In this third (transindividuational) moment what emerges is a collective knowing. It is, in Jung's terms, a deepening in the knowledge of the Self.

[I]ndependently of, and sometimes in direct contrast to, the outward forms they may take, [archetypes] represent the life and essence of a nonindividual psyche. Although this psyche is innate in every individual it can neither be modified nor possessed by him personally. It is the same in the individual as it is in the crowd and ultimately in everybody. It is the precondition of each individual psyche, just as the sea is the carrier of the individual wave.

(Jung, 1946, §354)

Alternative Approaches to the Phenomenon

What I have attempted to describe here is a dimension of the overall analytic process. As I have indicated, it should not be viewed reductively as an intrapsychic development within either party. Some Jungians have sought to understand such processes in terms of the "wounded healer" archetype. David Sedgwick, for example, observes that the analyst can sometimes be wounded by the patient on a sufficiently deep level such that "it is as if the unconscious wanted to bring the patient's wounds directly into the analytic situation, or induce an empathic reality entirely in the therapeutic 'here and now'" (1994, p. 109). As Sedgwick points out, this phenomenon puts what is occurring "beyond empathy" and indeed beyond a model that utilizes ideas of projection/introjection/projective identification. However, although Sedgwick offers some fascinating and insightful detail in his real-time accounts of these dynamics as they show up in analysis, he pulls back from offering a satisfying theoretical explanation for what occurs, suggesting cautiously that Dieckmann's invocation of ESP or parapsychology might provide the "best current explanation" (1994, p. 116).

If, however, we are seeking a firmer theoretical basis for such phenomena, my suggestion is that we need look no further than Jung's own archetypal psychology—so long as we view it on the transindividual level. All the phenomena Sedgwick describes (alongside Dieckmann's examples of synchronicity in analysis (1976)) as well as other well-known phenomena such as revelatory supervision (whereby analyst returns to the patient after supervision to find that certain transformations have occurred) relate to this "third" region that transcends and contains analyst and analysand qua individuals and within which transformation occurs. As I have argued, this field can *only* be constellated on a collective level, beyond either of the individuals involved, even though, paradoxically, it will continue to feel as though the changes are experienced subjectively as deeply personal and intimate.

What Sedgwick does note is that, at its most healing and creative, the field shows up as a *coniunctio*: "a fused, eros-oriented style of experience" (Sedgwick, 1994, p. 115). He sees this as a deep "mutual identification" whereby infection and detoxification between the participants takes place directly on the "wounded levels" of both, such that "the therapist is made 'sick' by the patient … The former then cures himself and thereby cures the patient" (Sedgwick, 1994, p. 117). This is a rich and, in some ways, accurate description but because it concentrates upon analyst and patient as separate individuals it omits the crucial *collective* dimension of what is occurring.

Some psychoanalytic literature (e.g. Searles or Bion) also acknowledges the manifestation of phenomena like this. However, limitations in the underlying psychological model require them to be understood in terms of the patient identifying with and then introjecting the fruits of the analyst's self-analysis. As an explanation, this seems strikingly and unnecessarily contrived.

Implications for Clinical Practice

The positing of an archetypal/collective field that operates autonomously within analysis points to the necessity for an adjusted understanding of the role of the analyst within the process. The skill of the analyst now shows up, not so much in controlling or guiding the analysis via amplifications and interpretations, but rather by staying in touch with the elusive affective relational shifts that are constantly in motion (Jung, 1946, §384) and thus facilitating the transformative dimension of the process. This attitude requires something like Bion's abnegation of "desires for results, 'cure' or even understanding" (Bion, 1990, p. 244). In order to serve the process/field through "not knowing", the analyst is required to take a step back not only from the role of one-that-knows (Lacan) but also from the status of analyst qua constituted individual. Had Jung been busily interrogating his own countertransference he might well have missed the insect tapping at the window. No synchronicity, no field, and therefore no transformation of the field would then have occurred. Sufficient breathing space for the expression and observation of the full gamut of relational vectors in the room will only occur when the analyst can allow herself to be attended by the wider collective process (or in Keats' words, by "negative capability" (Keats, 1899, p. 277)).

As we saw in the clinical example from Schwartz-Salant, the analyst's responsibility is not only to guard against numerous potential avenues of avoidance, but also to gently enable both analyst and patient to stay where the field shows up at its most awkward and intense. If any healing emerges, it should be seen not as an achievement of either analyst or analysand, but as a "third" archetypal/collective dimension that has emerged out of and transcended the process. This "cure" may affect both parties, but it actually operates outside of the personal/individual agenda. Clearly, there is a strong aspect of mutuality here, but it is ultimately a secondary product of the shared nature of the field within which multiple relational vectors are active.

It is important also to emphasize that although these vectors seem to occur in both personal/individual and archetypal/collective dimensions, it is the interaction between the two that constellates meaning in the most transformative way. If either approach dominates the interpretive attitude, then it will fail, either because it becomes one-sidedly personal (bringing with it the danger of acting-out) or because it becomes excessively vague, intellectual, and disembodied. From this perspective, the real skill of the analyst is to sense which level of analysis, which dimension of the relational field, is asking to be focused upon at any one moment, and, simultaneously, to take the whole into account.

Perhaps not surprisingly, such work is similar to dream-work. Within analysis, the dream is a shared, whole image that, as we have seen, is constellated from and within the field between analyst and patient. It is this wholeness (of image and of field) that informs the way detailed attention is paid to any specific imaginal facets, personal associations, or amplifications. If both the individual aspects and the collective aspects can be held in syzygy, the dream, as a third, will—as it were—interpret itself, and in this way the whole image can speak to the whole field. Far from being detached or abstract, interpretive work of this kind is profoundly relational and affectively situated. It comes to life only when held within a whole network of active relational vectors.

From this perspective, the primary quality of an archetypal process can be said to reside in its overall capacity to transgress the limits of a solely personal/individual level of operation and thus achieve transindividuality. The capacity to evoke specific "archetypal" or symbolic/mythological material will always remain subsidiary to this overall capacity. This means that within analysis, the making of an archetypal/mythological interpretation or amplification can never, in itself, constellate or even necessarily point to the presence of a living archetypal process. On the contrary, such a gesture will very often enact an avoidance of the collective/archetypal field.

Although these moments in analysis are frequently colored by a certain level of affective intensity, we need to beware of understanding this intensity in solely personal terms. Such intensity points to an engagement with the shared collective dimension of life. Victor Turner uses the word "communitas" to describe the intense intimacy that develops among persons in a group entering a zone of liminality (1969). Unlike participation mystique, communitas "does not merge identities; the gifts of each person are alive to the full, along with those of every other person" (Salamone, 2004, p. 98). To inhabit communitas is then to entertain a transindividuational tension between the purely personal and the purely collective, simultaneously archetypal and intimate.

Although we have focused here upon the way in which the transindividual emerges within analytic work, it can be also observed in other settings. The theatrical event, for example, offers an excellent illustration of the kind of relational intimacy I am attempting to describe. Just like analyst and patient, both audience and performers meet on several different levels. The actors are operating a) on the ordinary ego level (remembering their lines, adapting to lost props or misfitting costumes), b) on a deeper but personal level (caught up with their individual roles), and c) on the collective level (working as a unit, responding to and creating the play as a whole). At the same time, the audience members are also engaged on three different but related levels: a) individually (e.g. observing other audience members or reading the program), b) personally (e.g. being emotionally affected by those moments in the play that echo events in their own lives), and c) cohering as a unit (e.g. reacting en-masse and thereby participating in the playing out of the whole drama). This third, transindividual level of engagement constitutes a conjoined field within which actors and audience together occupy a creative and resonant tension. This (Dionysian) dimension of experience is at the core of the theatrical event. It simply cannot be perceived or described within the limited terms of individual psychology. The relational complexity of the theatrical event (and particularly its capacity to operate simultaneously on both individual and collective levels) provides a close parallel to the relational dynamic we find constellated, in a different way, in analysis.

Conclusion

Jung's careful scrutiny of the relational vectors that show up in analytic work clarifies some of the complex ways in which these lines of relation operate intrapsychically and interpersonally. This contribution alone provides an important elaboration of what can only be described as a relational psychology. I have, however, tried to argue here that Jung's writings on transference go much further than this. Jung gives us an account of the emergence of a "third" field that operates autonomously within the analytic vessel. This operation occurs on a collective (archetypal) level that transcends the limitations of the individual psyche but without falling back into a state of symbiosis, merger, or "participation mystique." Jung thus adumbrates the notion of a wider individuation that transcends the separate individuations of the constituted individuals within the analytic relationship. This transindividuation, as Simondon has characterized it, emerges, in theoretical terms, out of various radical implications of Jung's late psychology, such as synchronicity, the *Unus Mundus*, and the psychoid. However, by exploring the clinical application, Jung grounds these notions in the detailed to-and-fro of everyday analytic work. Despite his general tendency to focus on the individual and the intrapsychic Jung here points toward the potential emergence of a truly relational psychology. If, however, we want to take seriously the radical nature of Jung's ideas about the psyche, we must begin to re-vision what we mean by the relational. By focusing here upon this collective (archetypal) dimension of relationality I have, I hope, made a start.

Notes

1 Gilbert Simondon's ideas are particularly useful when applying constructive critical thinking to Jung since his rigorous attempt to think the relational occurs within an overall focus upon the process of individuation. In brief, Simondon takes up Jung's notion of the individuation process and places it at the centre of a radical and wide-reaching theory of onto-genesis. Although Simondon's ideas are fascinating in their own right, and reward deep study, most are tangential to the subject of this chapter.

2 Jung's original diagram refers specifically to anima-animus and the so-called mar-
   riage quaternio, here it has been applied more generally to the dynamics of trans-
   ference/countertransference as he describes them in the same work.

References

Aron, L. (1996). *A Meeting of Minds: Mutuality in Psychoanalysis.* Analytic.

Benjamin, J. (1999). Afterword. In S. A. Mitchell & L. Aron (Eds.), *Relational Psychoanalysis: The Emergence of a Tradition* (pp. 201–210). Routledge.

Benjamin, J. (2004). Beyond doer and done to: An intersubjective view of thirdness. *Psychoanalytic Quarterly*, 73, 5–46.

Bion, W. R. (1990). Notes on memory and desire. In R. Langs (Ed.), *Classics in Psychoanalytic Technique* (pp. 243–244). Jason Aronson. (Original work published 1967).

Brown, R. S. (2017). Where do minds meet? Mutual recognition in light of Jung. In R. S. Brown (Ed.), *Re-encountering Jung: Analytical Psychology and Contemporary Psychoanalysis.* Routledge.

Burkitt, I. (1997). Social relationships and emotions. *Sociology*, 31(1), 37–55.

Cambray, J. (2004). Synchronicity as emergence. In J. Cambray & L. Carter (Eds.), *Analytical Psychology: Contemporary Perspectives in Jungian Analysis.* Brunner-Routledge.

Cambray, J. (2012). *Synchronicity, Nature and Psyche in an Interconnected Universe.* Texas A&M University Press.

Civitarese, G. (2022). *Psychoanalytic Field Theory: A Contemporary Introduction.* Routledge.

Clough, P. (Ed.) (2007). *The Affective Turn: Theorizing the Social.* Duke University Press.

Colman, W. (2013). Bringing it all back home: How I became a relational analyst. *Journal of Analytical Psychology*, 58, 470–490.

Combes, M. (2013). *Gilbert Simondon and the Philosophy of the Transindividual.* MIT Press.

de Moura, V. (2014). Learning from the patient: The East, synchronicity and transference in the history of an unknown case of C. G. Jung. *Journal of Analytical Psychology*, 59(3), 391–409.

Dieckmann, H. (1976). Transference and countertransference: Results of a Berlin research group. *Journal of Analytical Psychology*, 21(1), 25–35.

Giegerich, W. (2010). The end of meaning and the birth of man. In W. Giegerich, *The Soul Always Thinks: Collected English Papers, Vol. 4.* Spring Publications.

Huskinson, L. (2006). Holy, holy, holy: The misappropriation of the numinous in Jung. In A. Casement & D. Tacey (Eds.), *The Idea of the Numinous: Contemporary Jungian and Psychoanalytic Perspectives* (pp. 200–211). Routledge.

Jansen, D. B. (2003). *Jung's Apprentice: A Biography of Helton Godwin Baynes.* Daimon Verlag.

Jung, C. G. (1946). The psychology of the transference. In C. G. Jung, *Collected Works, Vol.* 16 (paras. 353–539). Princeton University Press.

Jung, C. G. (1952). Synchronicity: An acausal connecting principle. In C. G. Jung, *Collected Works, Vol.* 8 (paras. 816–967). Princeton University Press.

Jung, C. G. (1959). Good and evil in analytical psychology. In C. G. Jung, *Collected Works, Vol.* 10 (paras. 858–886). Princeton University Press.

Jung, C. G. (1961). Symbols and the interpretation of dreams. In C. G. Jung, *Collected Works, Vol.* 18 (paras. 416–617) Princeton University Press.

Jung, C. G. (1973). *Letters, Vol.* 1. Princeton University Press.

Jung, C. G. (2009). *Liber Novus.* W. W. Norton & Company.

Jung, C. G. & Jaffé A. (1989). *Memories, Dreams, Reflections.* Vintage Books.

Keats, J. (1899). *The Complete Poetical Works and Letters of John Keats, Cambridge Edition.* Houghton, Mifflin & Co.

Main, R. (2007). Synchronicity and analysis: Jung and after. *European Journal of Psychotherapy and Counselling,* 9(4), 359–371.

Main, R. (2013). Myth, synchronicity and re-enchantment. In L. Burnett, S. Bahun & R. Main (Eds.), *Myth, Literature and the Unconscious* (pp. 129–146). Karnac Books.

Massumi, B. (2015). *Politics of Affect.* Polity.

Ogden, T. H. (2004). The analytic third: Implications for psychoanalytic theory and technique. *Psychoanalytic Quarterly,* 73.

Saban, M. (2016). Jung, Winnicott and the divided psyche. *Journal of Analytical Psychology,* 61(3), 329–349.

Saban, M. (2019). *'Two Souls Alas': Jung's Two Personalities and the Making of Analytical Psychology.* Chiron Press.

Salamone, F. A. (Ed.) (2004). *Encyclopedia of Religious Rites, Rituals and Festivals.* Routledge.

Samuels, A. (2012, unpublished). "The Analyst is as Much 'in the Analysis' as the Patient" (1929): Jung as a Pioneer of Relational Psychoanalysis.

Schwartz-Salant, N. (1988). Archetypal foundations of projective identification. *Journal of Analytical Psychology,* 33.

Schwartz-Salant, N. (1998). *The Mystery of Human Relationship.* Routledge.

Searles, H. F. (1973). Concerning therapeutic symbiosis. *Dynamische Psychiatrie,* 6(6), 373–390.

Searles, H. F. (1975). The patient as therapist to his analyst. In H. F. Searles, *Countertransference and Related Subjects.* International Universities Press.

Sedgwick, D. (1994). *The Wounded Healer: Counter-Transference from a Jungian Perspective.* Routledge.

Sedgwick, D. (2026). *Jungian Analysis and Relational Psychoanalysis: An Integration.* Routledge. Forthcoming.

Simondon, G. (2020). *Individuation in Light of Notions of Form and Individuation.* University of Minnesota Press.

Turner, V. W. (1969). *The Ritual Process: Structure and Antistructure.* Aldine.

Chapter 2

Some Implications of Synchronicity and the Psychoid for Analytical Psychology

Joe Cambray

Analytical psychology is rooted in healing from trauma associated with a divided self. For the founder, C. G. Jung, recovery was predicated on holding and enduring the tension of the opposites with subsequent resolution through the emergence of a third position transcendent to the conflict. There is a mechanistic quality to this vision with its required discrimination of opposites as the only path to consciousness (Jung, 1954, para. 178). Stated in the abstract the task leans towards an intrapsychic pathway for the development of consciousness. This has been identified as arising out of Jung's own struggle with his divided self, articulated in terms of his number 1 and 2 personalities (Saban, 2019). While he acknowledges every psychology is a personal confession, including his own, the impact on his theory and practices of potential biases was not often identified or articulated. This chapter will look at and assess how Jung, in collaboration with Wolfgang Pauli, attempted to apply an Hegelian logic of transcending opposites to the matter–spirit dichotomy in western thought, formulating the notion of the psychoid archetype to give a theoretical base for the synchronicity hypothesis. The relational and psychosocial dimensions of their hypotheses were only briefly, if at all, touched upon. Here I will seek to explore a more expanded view of the problem and consider some undeveloped implications.

An appreciative, yet critical review of Jung's orientation to opposites was offered by philosopher James Jarrett in 1989 following the publication of the two-volume set of Jung's seminars on Nietzsche's *Zarathustra*, which he had just edited (Jarrett, 1989). Examining Jung's comments such as "in [the unconscious] the opposites slumber side by side" (Jung, 1955, para. 184), Jarrett notes that "though the conflict of opposites is clearly of great importance, are there not other kinds of realization that are the concomitants of growing consciousness?" (Jarrett, 1989, p. 67). Using the sequential development of language in children as an example he goes on to observe, "Is not this perception and realization of *similarities* just as much evidence of a new evolving consciousness as is the perception of *opposition*?" (Jarrett, 1989, p. 67, emphasis in original). He also suggests that like opposites, similars must lie in proximity in the unconscious. This leads to a more sequential model: "the ideal is to move from awkward, blurred,

DOI: 10.4324/9781003429142-2

lumpish functioning towards easy, sharp discriminated functioning" (Jarrett, 1989, p. 69). I imagine Jung might agree with some aspects of this modulation of his stance but would be drawn back toward a more polarized view when deeper levels of the unconscious are activated.

What neither Jarrett nor Jung focus on is the role of caretakers in the evolution of consciousness. The mind does not emerge solely through intrapsychic processes but is at its base relational. While not in the forefront of Jung's theorizing, a radical relationality can be found in some of Jung's correspondence, such as when supervising James Kirsch on a patient's transference dreams: "With regard to your patient, it is quite correct that her dreams are occasioned by you ... In the deepest sense we all dream not out of ourselves but out of what lies between us and the other" (Jung, 1973, p. 172).

As a pioneer in the psychology of the unconscious Jung's writings are peppered with intuitions and insights, a number of which have been left to future generations to flesh out. In some places this reflects the limitations of the intellectual milieu of his time (e.g., on complex systems), in other cases the limitations of his personal interests. Clearly Jung was not a monolithic thinker, nor did he always concern himself with fully articulating his theories.

Where Jung may be most engaging for contemporary readers is at the edges of his ideas. Though often shrouded in uncertainty these are the places where links to the future are most lively, including 21st-century insights that confirm or modify and expand on his thinking. The present chapter is written in this spirit.

The Use of Complexity Theory and Emergence

As I have written in various places, the approach to the world offered by complexity theory provides an avenue into Jung's most innovative conceptualizations revealing their profound visionary qualities. This began for me with re-visioning synchronicity in terms of emergence (Cambray, 2002). This movement to incorporate complexity into analytical psychology was significantly advanced by a pioneering paper authored by David Tresan on Jung's metapsychology (1996). Others soon applied this thinking to complexes, archetypes, and transference: Hogenson (2001), Saunders and Skar (2001), Knox (2003), Martin-Vallas (2008), Merchant (2019), and many others offered valuable contributions. Linda Carter and I also suggested that much of Jung's implicit methodology for working with unconscious material could be seen as an intuitive search for the emergent (Cambray & Carter, 2004).

To the extent that Jung intuitively moved towards insights that would foreshadow the conception of emergence in a richer systemic sense of the term, he seems to have been groping towards a way to transcend the theory of opposites. He was hampered by his anxieties about social and group dynamics, seeing them as almost wholly negative. This prejudice foreclosed recognition of the emergent properties of multiagent systems and the wisdom that can be discovered in groups. Nevertheless, the seeds of emergence are to be seen in his views on transcending the opposites. A particularly powerful example is found in *The Red Book* where he intuitively captures the optimal conditions for systemic emergence (at the edge of order and chaos): "If you marry the ordered to the chaos you produce the divine child, the supreme meaning beyond meaning and meaninglessness" (2009, p. 139n).

In pioneering research into the origins of life on earth, theoretical biologist Stuart Kauffman (1993) employed the complex adaptive systems perspective which includes the possibility of spontaneous self-organization to model the condition for life's emergence. In brief, his results point to the conditions for this emergence as most likely to occur at the edge of order and chaos. This locus of dynamic emergence was further explored and applied to various systems by numerous others associated with the Santa Fe Institute in New Mexico, which has become the leading institution of complexity research. Applying this logic to clinical dyads allows a reexamination of synchronistic phenomena associated with the analytic process to be grasped in terms of complex adaptive systems, as I discussed in my initial paper on the topic (Cambray, 2002). However, the frame can remain locked in a dyadic configuration with the synchronistic phenomenon appearing as a supervening third which does not explicitly challenge the opposition model. Jung's paradigmatic case is that of the woman with a "highly polished Cartesian rationalism" who reported a dream of being given a piece of golden jewelry in the shape of a scarab beetle at the moment Jung heard a tapping at his consulting room window, whereupon he opened the window and caught a rose chafer beetle which he then handed to her. This remarkable coincidence was understood by Jung to break through her rational defenses and open a pathway for the analysis to proceed. This is framed as an opposition of her rationality to his having "confined myself to the hope that something unexpected and irrational would turn up" (Jung, 1954, para. 962). Nevertheless, even in this case, when we consider his own prior history as revealed near the beginning of *The Red Book* of the solar hero in the waters of the unconscious pursued by a monstrous beetle, we can glimpse that there may have indeed been unreported counter-transference mobilized by the client's dream image, which harkened back to some traumatic memories for Jung. Looked at from an interactive field perspective, shared dynamics seem at play which when considered as a part of the whole, diminish the extent of overt polarization. Might the patient's resistance to the unconscious have constellated a counter-reaction which the shared synchronistic phenomena broke through for both parties? The suggestion here is that a more interactive view may have decreased the degree of polarization from opposition toward co-creation while permitting a mutual experience of awe in the manifestation of the psyche in the consulting room.

As discussed in my initial paper on synchronicity (Cambray, 2002), the case of the "Black Forest" was marked by a synchronicity from my analytic practice. The client had dreamt of being unable to find me in the Black Forest while I was away on a trip. In a scheduled phone session, she immediately, with great anxiety, asked if I were in Germany and explained the question by reporting the dream. While I was in fact in the Caribbean, I realized the abandonment distress occasioned by my absence and so worked to successfully address this. However, the next day when I unexpectedly went for my first dive in open water, I discovered with considerable surprise the site was called the "Black Forest" for the rare black coral which lived on that portion of the reef. As a consequence of the remarkable, meaningful coincidence, a thorough reconsideration of the unconscious processes activated in the case was necessary. Using the complexity approach, I have been able to realize that the impact of the client's dream image, taken together with my dive, exhibited a bi-directionality of influence, moving my client toward a more organized state, while there was a back-reaction shifting me toward a more chaotic state. Taken as a whole, the therapeutic process had moved to the edge of order and chaos as the synchronicity manifested. The bi-directionality was not dynamically symmetrical—asymmetries remained in the way we each experienced the numinous—but it was effective for both participants as befitted our individual needs for proceeding with the analysis (Cambray, 2002). This was my paradigmatic case for re-visioning synchronicity in terms of complexity and emergence. In my Fay Lectures I also explored the appearance of synchronistic phenomena in historical situations that point toward socio-cultural dimensions in (some) synchronicities, moving beyond dyadic to multi-agent systems (Cambray, 2009).

From a theoretical standpoint, one premise of this chapter is that Jung's final framing of the archetypal realm in terms of psychoid qualities, required by the synchronicity hypothesis, offers a pathway toward a view of the psyche less dependent on polarization as a primary theoretical position. This was not fully realized by Jung as will be detailed below. Similarly, the link between the realm of the psyche and that of matter manifesting in synchronicities necessitates a more porous relationship between inner and outer worlds than had previously been identified. This in turn leads to a more ecologically-based view of the psyche, as will be discussed, including clinical and environmental ramifications.

Reconsidering the Psychoid Realm

In the effort to provide a theoretical frame for synchronistic phenomena, Jung employed his boldest vision of the archetypal world. This was accomplished through his coining of the "psychoid archetype," Jung's furthest theoretical stretch beyond his internal/psychologically biased view of archetypes. In formulating the psychoid archetype he leans more heavily toward inclusion of the realm of spirit, which within his metaphor of the light spectrum for psychological consciousness is located beyond or higher (in frequency) than our human vision/consciousness can perceive. He references the ultraviolet metaphor directly as follows: "The archetype as such is a psychoid factor that belongs, as it were to the invisible, ultraviolet end of the psychic spectrum. It does not appear, in itself, to be capable of reaching consciousness" (Jung, 1954, para. 417).

The omission of the physical dimension of reality, the infra-red aspect of the light spectrum (metaphorically representing the somatic and material aspects of the psyche) here is striking, though it does come in a bit later as we will see. However, when this does enter, the inability to reach consciousness is not reiterated or even mentioned. The implicit bias, favoring the spirit over the matter, points to a conflict I will examine more closely below in terms of what I refer to as the "psychoid imagination."

Before proceeding there, let's examine Jung's attempt to extend archetypal theory to include physical reality. In the paragraph of "On the Nature of the Psyche" that follows that just cited, Jung moves toward what has been termed a dual aspect monism according to the work of Atmanspacher and colleagues, including most recently a book co-authored with the historian of the philosophy of science, Dean Rickles (2022). While not explicitly stated in Jung's essay, the hypothesis of an *unus mundus*, as discussed in *Mysterium Con-iuntionis*, is envisioned as the unitary background, prior to any separation into psyche and matter. The *unus mundus* holds the holistic potential which can only be regained through the alchemical notion of the *mysterium con-iunctionis*, the topic and goal of Jung's last major work, which was first published in German in 1955–6 and subsequently translated into English several years after his death in 1961. Returning to "On the Nature of the Psyche", first presented in 1946, Jung had already looked toward a unitary factor:

> Since psyche and matter are contained in one and the same world, and moreover are in continuous contact with one another and ultimately rest on irrepresentable, transcendental factors, it is not only possible but fairly probable, even, that psyche and matter are two different aspects of one and the same thing. The synchronicity phenomena point, it seems to me, in this direction, for they show that the nonpsychic can behave like the psychic, and vice versa, without there being any causal connection between them. Our present knowledge does not allow us to do much more than compare the relation of the psychic to the material world with two cones, whose apices, meeting in a point without extension—a real zero-point—touch and do not touch.
>
> (Jung, 1954, para. 418)

In this passage, Jung elides any spirit/psyche differences, setting up a polarization of matter against the psyche/spirit; matter can only "behave like the psychic" but seems not to share in the archetypal the way that spirit does. However, he does go on to metaphorize the infrared end of the spectrum with the somatic pole of the mind-body question being more identified with instinct as differentiated from archetype. From the body he proceeds to link more generally with matter, though not quite with the same primacy as given to psyche/spirit for the archetype (Jung, 1954, para. 420).

In his final letter to Wolfgang Pauli in August 1957[1] Jung discussed the breakdown of symmetry in some microphysics experiments and their psychic parallel in a manner that suggests greater parity between psyche and matter, while ironically, acknowledging the value of asymmetry[2] "the psychoid archetype, [is] where 'psychic' and 'material' are no longer viable as attributes, or where the category of opposites becomes obsolete and every occurrence can only be asymmetrical" (Pauli et al., 2001, p. 169).

The dissolving of the framework of strict polarization here can be liberating as it would render the light spectrum metaphor more useful. Within that context Jung's argument from para. 418 would be akin to putting UV (and frequencies above this) together with visible light as the domain of the archetypes in opposition to infrared (and below) as the instinctual, material realm. There are of course no such sharp distinctions. These are simply useful human categories linked to our visual perception; "light" includes only a limited range of the full electromagnetic spectrum phenomena. By analogy I suggest the psychoid archetype unequivocally partakes of the full spectrum of phenomena, from spirit through matter.[3] Both light and the archetype can be perceived as holistic phenomena, not readily dissociable or reduced to functional parts.

An important ramification of moving beyond the spirit/matter polarity would be the possibility of envisioning the psyche more fully as an emergent property of the body/mind/world, arising from the interactions among multiple agents rather than just from a tension of opposites (dyadic structures). This would then facilitate viewing the psyche from an ecological perspective, seeing its embeddedness in the environments from which it arose, including the physical, biological, human, and spiritual. The psyche could then be recognized as manifesting various degrees of complexity based on levels of emergence available up to and including mind and spirit as well as extending further into sociological and cultural dimensions.

Synchronicities as manifestations of constellated psychoid archetypes could then be recognized at these various levels of psychic emergence. An intimation of this was suggested by Jung in response to Erich Neumann in their correspondence on synchronistic-like events occurring during the course of evolution. As I have noted before, Jung envisioned a psychoid process occurring "with which a physical event meaningfully coincides" in a "preconscious time" (2002, p. 418). He goes on to describe "unconscious synchronicities," stating "[t]hey point to a latent meaning which is independent of consciousness" (Jung, 1973, p. 495). The freeing of synchronicities from immediate, conscious meaning allows a more realistic reflection process, including the notion that meaning may not come to consciousness even within a lifetime, but remains latent. From this we might ask whether a historical analysis may assist us in locating psychoid phenomena, including (proto-) synchronistic events in the course of world affairs? If affirmed, we can then look at some psychosocial implications, but as a first step, we need to consider the idea of a psychoid aspect to the imagination.

The Psychoid Imagination

Jung's remarks on the psychoid presented above seem to rule out the possibility of becoming conscious of such events. It appears they would be above, or below, the range of conscious representation. However, there is evidence based on Jung's own images from his dreams and fever visions (when ill and recovering from a case of H1N1 flu in 1919)[4] that he may have intuited the morphology of the infecting agent and given it visual representation. As I have argued, the images Jung painted during his illness (found in Hoerni et. al., 2018) show signs of a somatic intuition about the form of the infecting agent (Cambray, 2023a, pp. 274–6). Since viruses are at the edge of the living world (they can be crystallized and stored without damage or need for energy input for extended periods similar to many pure, inorganic substances, yet remain virulent when reintroduced into the environment), in this sense they are the epitome of the psychoid realm. The shape of the infecting virus was not known for many years after the H1N1 pandemic was over, i.e., there were no scientific images of the infectious agent available during the time of Jung's paintings, so they were not based on external evidence.

Jung's eventual placing of the key image of a complex sphere in the branches of a tree, giving visual representation to the *lumen naturae* as depicted in Figure 131 of *The Red Book*, could be understood in terms of analogy to what is now known of the shape of the virus from which he was suffering in 1919 (Jung, 2009, p. 131). Further, the placement in the tree (a form of the philosophical tree) may be linked to the cultural malaise of the times, a disenchantment of the world (Cambray, 2023b). As I have argued this would be a powerful visual precursor to Jung's pronouncement that "the gods have become diseases" (Jung, 1967, para. 54). Here his visual metaphor could indicate that the disease has become the *lumen naturae* to show us a pathway towards reenchantment or as he would state it, respiritualization of the world. The incorporation of a profound intuition about a psychoid substance (the virus) into visual imagery proclaiming a fundamental philosophical change in the archetypal pattern of the western world suggests Jung's unrecognized capacities as a visual thinker and artist. The rather remarkable act of grasping an essential but unknown aspect of the external world through the imagination is not unique to Jung but can be found in a number of artists. They bring forward an aspect of the psyche not yet fully described or understood. For our purposes I will call this capacity or function the "psychoid imagination."

Several other illustrative examples can be given displaying intricate knowledge of the world beyond what is currently known to science or conscious understanding, but discovered retrospectively once such knowledge is available. Thus, from Islamic architectural tiling patterns we can consider the Alhambra in Granada, Spain, built by artisans of the Nasrid dynasty primarily in the period 1238 to 1358. The remarkable diversity of the patterns of tiling has recently been explored and discussed by mathematician Marcus du

Sautoy, a distinguished Professor of Mathematics at the University of Oxford, in his 2008 book *Symmetry: A Journey into the Patterns of Nature*. He confirms earlier studies that indicated all of the 17 mathematically possible crystallographic plane symmetry groups are represented on the walls. As some of these are not obvious, and indeed some mathematicians who have studied the Alhambra only found 14 groups (color patterns need to be included to locate all 17), the artisans of the 13th and 14th centuries who accomplished this appear to have had a remarkable intuition about the entire range of possible abstract patterns.

Another Islamic structure bearing amazingly complex tiling patterns is the Darb-e Imam mausoleum in Isfahan, Iran. While there is controversy about the time period in which the panels were constructed, it is argued that they manifest an aperiodic quasi-crystalline pattern which matches the "Penrose" pattern, discovered by cosmologist Prof. Roger Penrose in the 1970s. Although this pattern appears symmetrical at first glance, under close scrutiny it reveals full symmetry only at infinity. Construction using this design, whether in the 15th or 18th century, remains a marvel and again points to an apprehension of an aspect of nature not fully described in consciousness at the time (Lauwers, 2018). It can be seen as another feat of an objective use of the imagination.

More recently Jackson Pollock's drip paintings from the late 1940s have been shown to have an underlying fractal aesthetic (Taylor et. al., 1999). His visual presentations predate articulations by Benoit Mandelbrot who coined the term fractal in 1975 (translated into English in 1977). Similarly, contemporary reevaluation of some of Vincent van Gogh's paintings done during periods of psychic turbulence, such as "The Starry Night," also have captured an unanticipated feature beyond contemporary understanding, the visual essence of physical turbulence when assessed from the point of view of physics (Ball, 2006).

These examples provide anecdotal evidence that some artists and artisans have been able to render aspects of nature in their artworks that transcend the known (Cambray, 2016). The penetration of the veil of nature these examples offer can point us to a new way to appreciate the imagination with its noetic potential. I believe Jung began to pursue this in his reflections on J. B. Rhine's ESP experiments, as when he made the bold statement:

> the subject's answer is not the result of his observing the physical cards, it is a product of *pure imagination*, of "chance" ideas which reveal the structure of that which produces them, namely the unconscious ... and on account of its "irrepresentable" nature I have called it "psychoid."
> (Jung, 1954, para. 840, emphasis mine)

This "pure imagination" which is of a psychoid nature can provide objective information suggesting a previously underexplored degree of porosity between inner and outer worlds. It also seems synonymous with the true imagination of alchemy (*imaginatio vera*). In a similar fashion, Georg Nicolaus states "*Imaginatio vera* is precisely that which binds these two dimensions, the subjective and the objective, together" (2012, p. 105). This faculty is what I am referring to as the psychoid imagination.

Let's consider several possible consequences of such a formulation. First, the porosity and interpenetration of psychic and physical realms is of course part of the synchronicity hypothesis, which can be expanded into a more general notion of the psyche. An ecological view of the psyche beyond our inscapes follows immediately. Psyche would not be "enskulled," analogous to Daniel Siegel's views about the mind being not only associated with brain activity but embodied and relational (2017). Psyche then is an extended reality as well as being experienced internally by ego consciousness. When considered in terms of interpersonal relations, psyche can be seen to present in a field-like manner: distributed, non-local, with interactive gradients (of affect, memory, imagination, and so forth). Such fields are not only co-constructed by the psyches of participants but also include the surrounding world with its psychoid contributions. There are sociological and environmental consequences which can be considered in addition to the usual clinical observations. For all of these modalities, polarized opposites as the primary agents are no longer an adequate description but a complex adaptive system's model does allow more accurate modeling.

For my Black Forest case, noted above, the reference to a forest in Germany sharing the same name as a patch of black coral is remarkable linguistically and contributed to the surprise that tends to come with emergent phenomena (which most synchronicities are). In addition, however, both "Black Forests" have experienced degradation due to climate change. In retrospect, the abandonment issues which seemed solely of a personal nature and were the clinical focus at the time of the dream/diving synchronicity, might also contain an environmental alert emerging in what I term the "collective preconscious," e.g., the synchronicity also points to the lack of concern for the environmental abuse which was already underway at that time.

The Collective Preconscious and Reverie

The notion of a collective preconscious may be a useful addition to the lexicon of depth psychology to discuss matters which collectives (from groups to societies and cultures, to the conscious world) could address but do not, despite potential urgency. Ignored warnings, repressed for political, economic, and/or social concerns and fears, are just the most obvious aspect of what lies in the collective preconscious. These matters are often of a psychoid nature, involving inner activation about outer issues. For example, avant-garde concerns, for social justice, equity, environmental deterioration, and related matters, often involve systemic concerns that frighten or anger significant segments of the population, charging up the preconscious with pent-up affects about the world and other people; these can remain without conscious reflection to the detriment of societies. They can readily degrade into antithetical positions of irreconcilable opposition, facilitated by shadow projections, though this is not an automatic or certain fate. Instead, developing an appreciation of the dynamics of the collective preconscious including its psychoid qualities might begin to give us more tools to deescalate conflicts. As a start in this direction, I will suggest one function that might aid us: reverie.

Reverie is generally defined as "daydreaming"—being lost in thought or imagination—and has more recently been linked to the Default Mode Network in neuroscientific studies (e.g., Abraham, 2018). Historically treated as inefficient states, wasting time from an enlightenment perspective, reveries have found a more positive acceptance in some areas of depth psychology, linking to play and creativity. Bion's understanding of mother–infant dyadic communications has elevated reverie into a mind forming activity. Thomas Ogden extended this to use as a tool in analysis to get at unconscious contents and dynamics in the interactive field, starting with his book *Reverie and Interpretation* (1998). Subsequently there has been increasing interest in the subject: a Google Scholar search of "reverie" from 2020 to the present produced more than 16,100 articles. In the analytic world the potential use of reveries has tended to be centered on excavating emerging unconscious or preconscious material in the clinical setting with a nod to its creative aspects.

Reverie's relation to analytic intuition has been noted (Ribeiro, 2022), along with the various ways in which it may manifest pre-consciously for the therapist and, if attended to, can provide valuable information on the state of the interactive field. Appreciation of reveries has been based upon analytically attending to spontaneous thoughts, images, feelings, somatic activations, and an even more diffuse sense of disturbances of the field as having noetic value in exploration of the psyche. For example, in conducting a supervision seminar online I remarked on the feeling engendered by a glitch in the order of slides being presented. The comment was really a wondering about the gap, a reverie stimulated by an affective disturbance of the field, which subsequently manifested in a synchronistic breakdown of equipment for the presenter. After this person regained access to computer and internet, they rejoined the group and successfully explored the meaning of the disturbance in the context of the case presentation. My reverie had alerted us to an unspecified "mess" being omitted from the presentation, which ultimately proved to be an important regression in service of the self that was integral to the forward movement of the case.

As analysts from a variety of schools have noted, attending to reveries can initially feel quite awkward, as it communicates a seeming distraction from the overt contents being presented. Nevertheless, tolerating the uncertainty and discomfort associated with entering states of reverie can be rewarding. Thus, for example, noting the specific instant/situation in which a particular reverie began can lead to the emergence of unexpected new material. This unanticipated productivity is itself an indication of a preconscious attunement to the field. There is a subtle discipline in this activity as awareness of counter-transferential interference is necessary so as not to elevate every distraction into meaningful inference. With practice most therapists can recognize their internal signs of activation, which can then be reflected upon for the noetic potential of the material arising. Often these have a somatic element and suggest the psychoid imagination has been engaged. Might this be extended beyond the consulting room (actual or virtual) into the world?

Towards a Reenchantment of the World

When reveries are unexpectedly revelatory there is often a sense of wonder which accompanies the discovery. In therapy this sense of wonder can be productively shared and explored by the participants, even if it is asymmetrical, e.g., one partner may be sensing it more strongly than the other. In some cases when a significant insight emerges there may even be an experience of awe at the manifestation of the psyche. The recovery of the capacity for wonder and awe when cultivated and sustained in daily life can lead towards the sense of a reenchantment of the world. This need not only occur within the context of therapy but can become part of a more general eco-psychological practice. For me this reenchantment is one of the goals of the individuation process as implicitly found in Jung's experiences around *The Red Book*[5] and the occurrence of synchronistic phenomena.

If we can envision an animated nature with whom we can engage as an imaginal dialogue partner, then a large step in the direction of reenchantment can be taken. This could be viewed as an extension of the approach to be found in Jung's foreword to Richard Wilhelm's translation of the I-Ching, where he remarked:

> I made an experiment strictly in accordance with the Chinese conception: I personified the book in a sense, asking its judgment about its present situation, i.e., my intention to present it to the Western mind ... Why not venture a dialogue with an ancient book that purports to be animated?
>
> (Jung, 1970, para. 975)

We would need to personify at least some aspects of nature for the exercises I have in mind. Can we not grant psychic autonomy to nature, engaging it with our psychoid imagination? The purpose would not be to extract information, though that can be a valuable by-product, but to establish an empathic rapport. How then to ask nature questions which might generate meaningful responses?

The cultivation of states of reverie, exploring their noetic value, can be applied to use of the psychoid imagination. Verifiable synchronicities become markers of validation when this imagination is active. There are of course dangers in reading our wishes and desires into events, which is why I prefer to follow events over time and see how matters unfold before deciding on the veracity of experiences. Thus, in the previously mentioned synchronistic equipment failure during supervision, confirmation came in the form of the reporter's insight into the meaning of the breakdown at the precise moment it occurred. Significant initial affect was mobilized, with a temporary feeling of shame, followed by insight derived from exploring the question posed by the supervisor. This led to a deeper understanding of the presentation of the clinical material and the supervisee's relationship with the client. The supervisee could now affectively access the psychoid imagination allowing a restoration of electronic contact coupled with a more profound sense of meaning around what had been omitted.

When leading workshops on wonder, awe, and reenchantment, I have found a process that seems to facilitate dialoguing with nature. Memories of wonder in many people's lives center around experiences in nature, especially if they have lived in an environment that has given them some access to more pristine aspects of the natural world. Recontacting the emotional quality of these experiences can serve as a beginning place to enter a dialogue. Opening the imagination to the affectively engaging environment sets the stage for either asking an open question to this scene, e.g., asking what it needs/wants, or simply waiting and observing what occurs. Perhaps an animal, or a tree, or a rock will catch our attention. By focusing on this, allowing it to animate, contact can be made. Once this is established an active imagination type of dialogue can ensue. Allowing the autonomy of the imaginal forms to become more substantial—increasing their sensorial density—tends to enhance the quality of the experience and with it the noetic value of the encounter. Over time, the practice of such activity brings a growing sense of reenchantment.

Rather than being a return to enchantment, the assessment of the noetic quality of the dialogue is key to reenchantment as a kind of post-disenchantment. What is learned and gained should be an enhancement, an extension of our worldview. Contradictions with our current knowledge base need to be examined closely. While paradigm shifts are part of this exploration, old views should not be abandoned without careful, deep scrutiny. The reenchantment being suggested requires full engagement of our critical faculties, not simply indulging of wishes and desires for how we want our world to be.

Conclusion

Beginning with the problem of opposites in Jung's model of the psyche, with its significance for recovering from trauma, this chapter explored a reframing of his formulation in terms of complex adaptive systems. The analysis suggests a broader, more flexible understanding of psychic phenomena can thus be obtained. A multi-agent approach readily moves beyond reductive dyadic polarizations such as transference/countertransference dynamics framed exclusively in terms of projective identification, towards a field model. This approach would highlight emergent phenomena, endorsing a holistic conceptualization of the systems being studied. This also offers a new depth psychological entree into collective phenomena such as social and cultural activities. Jung's reticence about group dynamics can then be taken as a legitimate warning but not sufficient reason to avoid these activities. In contradistinction to his expressed concerns (mob psychology, governed by the lowest common denominator of psychological functioning) is the genuine wisdom that can be found in groups, especially when composed of experts, often in varying fields (Ratner et. al., 2023).

Rereading Jung's paradigmatic synchronicity case (of the scarab beetle) through the lens of an interactive field model opens reflections onto cultural dimensions of synchronicity and a reconsideration of the psychoid. In particular, introduction of the "psychoid imagination" brings enhanced clarity and focus to the alchemical notion of the *imaginatio vera*. Examples of the use of this psychic function by artists and artisans throughout history suggest it is part of our human endowment. Developing a disciplined approach to exploring the appearance and meanings of reveries could enhance access to aspects of the psyche that might otherwise be overlooked. Beyond the valuable clinical implications, this capacity also suggests a pathway out of our current cultural malaise of disenchantment. A re-visioning of Jung's suppositions about transcending the tension of opposites as an exclusive pathway to adult human development can strengthen the field and make analytical psychology more impactful for clinicians while expanding its utility for numerous other sociocultural and political endeavors. Are we prepared to take the next steps?

Notes

1   Several additional brief correspondences were made for Jung by Aniela Jaffe but without probing this matter further.
2   While not an explicit aspect of this argument, it should be noted that breaking symmetry is essential to increasing complexity: "the emergence of structures with increasing complexity…can be explained by cosmic phase transitions or symmetry breaking" (Mainzer 2007, p. 65).
3   The cosmology of the matter/spirit duality is woefully out of date. What are we to make of the fact that visible matter comprises only about 5% of the universe, with dark matter accounting for another 26 to 27% and the quite mysterious dark energy holding 68-69% of the total? A new cosmology is urgently needed to discuss archetypal patterns manifesting in "nature."
4   This was commonly known by the inaccurate label of the "Spanish flu," caused by a virus of the H1N1 type.
5   In a recent paper I argued that *The Red Book* provides evidence that Jung's view of individuation goes beyond a personal realization of the self, to an appreciation of synchronistic phenomena as part of the psychoid vision that would be incorporated into individuation (Cambray 2023b)

References

Abraham, A. (2018). The wandering mind: Where imagination meets conscious. *Journal of Consciousness Studies*, 25(11–12), 34–52.
Atmanspacher, H. and Rickles, D. (2022). *Dual-Aspect Monism and the Deep Structure of Meaning*. Taylor & Francis.

Ball, P. (2006). Van Gogh painted perfect turbulence. *Nature* (7 July). doi:10.1038/news060703-17

Cambray, J. (2002). Synchronicity and emergence. *American Imago*, 59(4), 409–434.

Cambray, J. (2009). *Synchronicity: Nature & Psyche in an Interconnected Universe* (Fay Lecture Series). Texas A & M University Press.

Cambray, J. (2016). Intuizione artistica e immaginazione psicoide: un ponte tra realta simboliche e ecologiche. *Enkelados*, 4, 117–133.

Cambray, J. (2023a). COVID-19, virtual engagement and the psychoid imagination. *Journal of Analytical Psychology*, 68(2), 272–280.

Cambray, J. (2023b). Reconsidering individuation in the 21st century: When archetypal patterns shift. In L. Sawin (Ed.), *Our Uncertain World: Challenges and Opportunities in a Dark Time*. Chiron Publications.

Cambray, J. and Carter, L. (2004). Analytic methods revisited. In J. Cambray and L. Carter (Eds.), *Analytical Psychology: Contemporary Perspectives in Jungian Psychology*. Brunner-Routledge.

Du Sautoy, M. (2008). *Symmetry: A Journey into the Patterns of Nature*. HarperCollins Publishers.

Hoerni, U., Fischer, T. and Baufmann, B. (Eds.) (2018). *The Art of C. G. Jung*. (Paul David Young and Christopher John Murray, Trans.). W. W. Norton & Co.

Hogenson, G. (2001). The Baldwin effect: A neglected influence on C. G. Jung's evolutionary thinking. *Journal of Analytical Psychology*, 46, 591–611.

Jarrett, J. L. (1989). Eros in the creation of consciousness: Nietzsche and Jung on the clash of opposites. *Psychological Perspectives*, 20(1), 62–71. doi:10.1080/00332928908407749

Jung, C. G. (1946). On the nature of the psyche. In C. G. Jung, *Collected Works, Vol. 8: Structure and Dynamics of the Psyche*, Princeton University Press.

Jung, C. G. (1954). Psychological aspects of the mother archetype. In C. G. Jung, *Collected Works, Vol. 9i: The Archetypes and the Collective Unconscious*, 2nd Ed., Princeton University Press.

Jung, C. G. (1955). *Mysterium coniunctionis*. In C. G. Jung, *Collected Works, Vol. 14*. Princeton University Press.

Jung, C. G. (1967). *Alchemical studies*. In C. G. Jung, *Collected Works, Vol. 13*. Princeton University Press.

Jung, C. G. (1970). Foreword to the I-Ching. In C. G. Jung, *Collected Works, Vol. 11*. Princeton University Press.

Jung, C. G. (1973). *Letters, Vol. 1: 1906–1950*. (Gerhard Adler and Aniela Jaffé, Eds.; R. F. C. Hull, Trans.). Routledge & Kegan Paul.

Jung, C. G. (1975). *Letters, Vol. 2: 1951–1961*. (Gerhard Adler and Aniela Jaffé, Eds.; R. F. C. Hull, Trans.). Princeton University Press.

Jung, C. G. (2009). *The Red Book*. (S. Shamdasani, Ed.). W. W. Norton & Co.

Kauffman, S. A. (1993). *The Origins of Order: Self-Organization and Selection in Evolution*. Oxford University Press.

Knox, J. (2003). *Archetype, Attachment, Analysis*. Brunner-Routledge.

Lauwers, L. (2018). Darb-e Imam tessellations: A mistake of 250 years. *Nexus Network Journal*, 20, 321–329.

Mainzer, K. (2007). *Thinking in Complexity: The Computational Dynamics of Matter, Mind, and Mankind*. 5th Ed. Springer-Verlag.

Mandelbrot, B. (1977). *Fractals: Form, Chance and Dimension*. W. H. Freeman & Co.

Martin-Vallas, F. (2008). The transferential chimera II: Some theoretical considerations. *Journal of Analytical Psychology*, 53(1), 37–59.

Merchant, J. (2019). An emergent/developmental model of archetype. *Journal of Analytical Psychology*, 64(5), 701–719.

Nicolaus, G. (2012). Schelling, Jung and the imaginatio vera. *International Journal of Jungian Studies*, 4(2), 104–120.

Pauli, W., Zabriskie, B., and Jung, C. G. (2001). *Atom and Archetype: the Pauli/Jung Letters, 1932–1958*. (C. A. Meier, C. P. Enz, and M. Fierz, Eds.; D. Roscoe, Trans.). Princeton University Press.

Ogden, T. (1998). *Reverie and Interpretation: Sensing Something Human*. Jason Aronson, Inc.

Ratner, N., Kagan, E., Kumar, P. and Ben-Gal, I. (2023). Unsupervised classification for uncertain varying responses: The wisdom-in-the-crowd (WICRO) algorithm. *Knowledge-Based Systems*, 272(110551), ISSN 950–7051. doi:10.1016/j.knosys.2023.110551 (https://www.sciencedirect.com/science/article/pii/S0950705123003015)

Ribeiro, M. F. da Rosa. (2022). The psychoanalytical intuition and reverie: Capturing facts not yet dreamed. *The International Journal of Psychoanalysis*, 103(6), 929–947. doi:10.1080/00207578.2022.2084402

Saban, M. (2019). *'Two Souls Alas': Jung's Two Personalities and the Making of Analytical Psychology*. Chiron Publications.

Saunders, P. and Skar, P. (2001). Archetypes, complexes and self-organization. *Journal of Analytical Psychology*, 46, 305–323.

Siegel, D. J. (2017). *Mind: A Journey to the Heart of Being Human*. W. W. Norton & Co.

Taylor, R., Micolich, A. and Jonas, D. (1999). Fractal analysis of Pollock's drip paintings. *Nature*, 399(422). doi:10.1038/20833

Tresan, D. (1996). Jungian metapsychology and neurobiological theory. *Journal of Analytical Psychology*, 41, 399–436.

Chapter 3

From Projection to Enactment in a Jungian Light

Robin S. Brown

As with many psychoanalytic concepts, a strict definition of enactment is difficult to pin down since the term has been used so variously. Broadly speaking, the idea of enactment reflects an effort to better understand the nature of unconscious communication and relatedness. While rising to prominence in the last 30 years, this line of thinking can be originally traced to Freud's concept of acting out.

Freud (1914) conceived of acting out as a defense mechanism where, in lieu of consciously remembering, the patient unconsciously performs some aspect of their past experience within the treatment. Despite the emphasis Freud placed on this process being a defensive operation opposed to conscious verbal formulation, he also recognized that it was possible to see the gesture of acting out as a form of communication. In fact, when we attempt to define what constitutes an unconscious action in contrast to a conscious verbalization it immediately becomes apparent that making a firm distinction between the two seems questionable. Perhaps in reaction to this potential lack of clarity, early Freudians tended to limit the meaning of acting out to emphasize thinking of this phenomenon as fundamentally defensive and with a particular accent on discrete observable behaviors.

The main factor differentiating enactment from acting out is the involvement of the analyst. While acting out is conceptually limited to the behaviors of the patient, enactment is understood as a shared performance involving patient and analyst wherein both participate in unconsciously dramatizing some aspect of the patient's interior life. To offer a brief example: a patient who was subject to broad indifference from their parents (but who is unable to confront this) might act out indifference in the treatment by consistently showing up late to sessions. While it might be expected that an attentive analyst would soon draw attention to this, suppose that the analyst appreciates the extra few minutes that the patient's lateness affords—say he quite enjoys the opportunity to peacefully drink his coffee and check his emails. Under such circumstances the analyst may find himself disinclined to draw attention to the emerging pattern, or perhaps he doesn't even notice it. The analyst has now fallen into performing the role of the disengaged parent and

DOI: 10.4324/9781003429142-3

we can more correctly speak of an enactment taking place rather than a simple case of acting out.

The foregoing example hopefully demonstrates how practical and heuristically useful these concepts are. At the same time, the relative clarity of the previous example is clearly somewhat misleading in that it leaves a number of questions unaddressed. What was happening in the treatment prior to the patient starting to show up late? Had the analyst already been withdrawing such that the enactment was already under way prior to the initial "acting out" on the part of the patient? What was it about the analyst's own experience that predisposed him to fall into this particular enactment? Is the patient's lateness perhaps triggering the analyst's own woundedness with respect to rejection?

Such questions have prompted many contemporary analysts to consider that enactment is best understood as an ongoing feature of the treatment (Katz, 2017)—that while the idea of a discrete enactment is often descriptively useful, the reality is a great deal more amorphous and difficult to circumscribe. Thus the psychoanalytic literature has moved from an early conception of acting out as a defensive process expressed in discrete and concrete behaviors, to a bewilderingly complex notion of enactment as a way of talking about the always-already situatedness of psychological life.

Relevance to Jungian Discourse

What points of connection can we initially establish between enactment theory and Jungian psychology? In so far as enactment has come to reflect a more relational approach to psychoanalysis, this evokes a broader question as to whether Jung can himself be considered a relational psychologist. While Jung's case material broadly speaking doesn't tend to highlight the role played by his own subjectivity, this stands in contrast with what we might loosely term his broader outlook and the ways in which he explicitly emphasizes the importance of the analyst's unique participation. Similarly, in contrast to the *unus mundus* sensibility that shows up in Jung's more speculative work or the radically relational sensibility often suggested in "The Psychology of the Transference" (Jung, 1946), in a more plainly clinical context the "collectivity" of the collective unconscious can sometimes seem limited to a phylogenetically shared inheritance of archetypes. In this fashion, an impression is sometimes given that the *collective* unconscious is in practice siloed into *individuals*.

There is a clear tension in Jung's work between the breadth of his thinking versus his efforts to make himself intelligible to a general scientific audience. As we have just seen in considering the psychoanalytic notions of acting out and enactment, the more clear and practical we are in defining our psychological concepts the more that tends to get left out in the process. Jung's efforts to make his work acceptable to a wider audience perhaps required that certain aspects of his thinking be minimized or "hinted at" rather than integrated into the substance of his approach to the clinical situation. In keeping with this, Jung's clinical ethos in print tends to express a conventional Cartesianism, even as the synchronistic paradigm rests upon dual-aspect monism.

The "isolated-mind" (Stolorow & Atwood, 1992) Cartesianism of Jung's day is perhaps evidenced most clearly with the extent to which Jung's practical psychology leans on the idea of projection. In contrast to the Freudian notion of projection understood as a defense mechanism, for Jung projection assumes broader significance and is fundamentally tied to our ability to perceive and engage with the world. Significantly, Jung often tends to conceptualize projection as the first step in bringing an unconscious content towards consciousness. Jung (1946, para. 383) writes: "the content can never be found and integrated directly, but only by the circuitous route of projection. For as a rule the unconscious first appears in projected form." Given the practical importance this notion has for Jung, it can be considered fundamental to how Jungians have approached clinical work.

What are the implications for the role played by projection in a Jungian clinical approach? Jung characterizes projection as an extroverted phenomenon wherein unconscious contents move towards consciousness by way of our (mis-)perception of the external environment. Yet it can be argued that the psychology of projection offered by Jung is itself biased towards introversion, for it often leads to a sense that the psyche is fundamentally located "within" individuals and thus can be encountered only at a delusional remove in relationship to the "outside" world (see Brown, 2014). In the extent to which Jung proposes a way out of this it is only by mastering the fundamentally introverted process of active imagination. The one-sided bias implicit in this psychology becomes clear when, for example, Marie Louise von Franz (1980, p. 34) states: "Introverted and introspective people can, however, perceive events in the inner world directly, without the detour of a projection onto an outer object." The "individuation of analytical psychology", as Saban (2019) has convincingly argued, clearly requires that this kind of typological one-sidedness be addressed.

Jung tends to foreground the question of mis-recognition attendant to projection while minimizing the importance of the "hook" upon which he says our projections are inevitably hung. This relates to a significant line of criticism within the relational literature with respect to Freudian orthodoxies and the propensity for authoritarianism that often arises from adopting a one-person psychology. Buirski (2005, p. 12) writes:

Mechanisms like reaction formation, projection, displacement and internalization presume that one self-contained, isolated mind can move some of its contents to another self-contained, isolated mind or take them in as if they were a foreign body. The problem is that while these constructs may be powerful pictorial metaphors, some theories treat them as if they were real mechanisms. By failing to capture the exquisitely context sensitive and mutually influencing processes at work, these metaphors influence clinical work by shaping how we understand and treat the person.

The danger of authoritarianism is evident in the history of analytical psychology in terms of the idea that an "analyzed person" has effectively withdrawn more of their projections and is thus more conscious or capable of being objective than the uninitiated. A framework of this nature only aggravates the dangers of psychic inflation attendant to analytic work. A more relational understanding might suggest that the analytic experience is about learning to be in a process rather than the idea of coming out the other side.

The introverted one-sidedness implicit in the psychology of projection is made further apparent where this line of thinking threatens to devalue the perceived authenticity and meaningfulness of our relationships. In a passage with a strongly relational cast, Jung (1946, para. 454) writes:

> The unrelated human being lacks wholeness only through the soul, and the soul cannot exist without its other side, which is always found in a "You." Wholeness is a combination of I and You, and these show themselves to be parts of a transcendent unity whose nature can only be grasped symbolically.

In a footnote, however, Jung (1946, para. 454) immediately undermines the strength of this passage by asserting:

> I do not, of course, mean the synthesis or identification of two individuals, but the conscious union of the ego with everything that has been projected into the "You." Hence wholeness is an intrapsychic process which depends essentially on the relation of one individual to another.

Jung (1946, para. 454) goes on to state:

> Although the possibility of gross deception is infinitely greater here that in our perception of the physical world, we still go on naively projecting our own psychology into our fellow human beings. In this way everyone creates for himself a series of more or less imaginary relationships based essentially on projection.

The threat of solipsism with this outlook is obvious. Jung's efforts to address this are reflected in certain corrective measures he employs such as the notions of passive projection and kinship libido. Indeed, there are times where Jung goes so far in nuancing his theory of projection that it becomes questionable whether we are still operating within the same paradigm—this is evident, for example, where he goes so far as to state that projection should be understood as a "subtle body" phenomenon (Jung, 1988, p. 1495). Roger

Brooke (1991, p. 57) observes that the concept of projection reflected an ongoing problem for Jung: "Throughout his work there are remarks about the importance of withdrawing projections from the world, together with a discussion of the fateful significance of doing so."

This whole topic relates to Jung's problematic relationship with "the primitive" wherein he vacillates between elevating indigenous people and equating them with children. Brooke (1991, p. 59) goes on to say: "Somehow, and I think this is crucial, a way needs to be found to understand our vital engagements within the life-world symbolically without spatialising that understanding and hauling psyche out of the world."

I would like to suggest that an important step in this direction has been offered by the extensive psychoanalytic literature on the subject of enactment. As we shall see, however, for the possibilities of this framework to be made more apparent requires a conception of the collective unconscious that has not been available to most relational analysts. A thoroughgoing relational approach requires a relational conception of psyche—that is, a transpersonal conception of psyche in the world, rather than one confined to isolated individuals.

Towards a Jungian Conception of Enactment

A particularly significant contribution to our thinking about enactment has been offered in the work of prominent relational analysts Galit Atlas and Lew Aron. Atlas and Aron (2018, p. 137) have been explicit in identifying the need of, as they put it, "a return of the 'soul,' of the 'psyche,' of soulfulness and spirit back to psychology." They also contend (2018, p. 153): "Intersubjectivity is not a joining of separate subjects but rather precedes and is the ground for it. On a deep unconscious level, we are always already interconnected and at one." Such claims will of course resonate strongly with many Jungians. In fact, in the years prior to his passing in 2019, Lew Aron was engaged extensively with Jung's ideas—reading him widely, referring to him often, and even running study groups to discuss Jung's works. As one of the most influential figures within the relational community, Aron's late work with his partner Galit Atlas emphasizes the question of teleology and in this fashion attempted to bring a significant line of Jungian influence into the psychoanalytic mainstream.

Atlas and Aron (2018, p. 13) argue that we should consider enactive process as inherently creative:

> We are suggesting ... that the flow of enactive engagement, the enactive dimension of analysis, may at times be fecund and transformative in and of itself, not only by working one's way out of it. Our argument for generative enactment is tied to and builds on our assumption that enactments dramatize, bring to life, not only the individual's conflicts but the intersubjective field, allowing for its growth and transformation through dramatic dialogue.

With this notion of *dramatic dialogue*, Atlas and Aron conceptualize a state of mind that facilitates the analyst's participation in the play of the therapeutic session. They underscore the need both of remaining watchful for the ways in which enactment may obstruct the analytic process, and for the ways in which we may prematurely interpret our experience thus preventing the necessary elaboration in analytic play.

By foregrounding a teleological/constructive approach to enactment, Atlas and Aron take a significant step towards outlining a Jungian approach to relational analytic encounter. A second necessary step requires that we broaden the scope of our thinking about enactment to move beyond the consultation room. Attending more to enactment as it occurs in the world outside treatment may help us appreciate the basis for Atlas and Aron's (2018) Jung-inflected claim that psychoanalytic ideas about enactment require a concept of soul (a claim that they make suggestively but don't actually expand upon). Because the understanding of enactment has arisen within the carefully circumscribed environs of the clinical setting, our impressions of this phenomenon may have been correspondingly truncated.[1]

The boundary of the analytic frame has enabled close attention to be paid to the ways in which the intrapsychic lives of two individuals—patient and analyst—can find points of resonance and intersection. However, the controlled nature of the clinical setting has tended to support a belief in what might be termed an "additive" approach to enactment—enactment has been understood in terms of events that are expressive of the intrapsychic life of the patient *plus* the intrapsychic life of the analyst (see Katz, 2017). The general assumption seems to be that the patient unconsciously draws the analyst into performing with the patient some aspect of the patient's past experience. This process is thought to work by means of an unconscious resonance with the analyst's own internal world triggered via something like projective identification or a related concept of inducement.

Stephen Mitchell (1984) has been influential in seeking to explain the continuity of a person's life experiences in terms of ongoing modes or relationship so as to avoid leaning too heavily on conceptions of frozen development, but an implicit Cartesian metaphysic (see Brown, 2017) prevents him from going far enough and leads to his approach placing an excessive emphasis on the *individual's* role in maintaining their own struggles. Crucially, this approach fails to account for the synchronistic dimension in experience, and the patient is excessively burdened with orchestrating their experience of the world. The refusal of a more "paranoid" attitude towards life (i.e. meaningful coincidence) results in a paranoid attitude being directed towards patients, this being reflected in a reliance on ideas that subtly betray an attitude of judicial suspicion—i.e. *inducement*, or to use Wachtel's (2008) term *accomplices*, by which he means that we unconsciously seek out other people who will conform with our expectations. It might be asked to what extent this way of thinking really moves beyond classical assumptions? Approaches of this kind still imply an encapsulated model of mind, albeit with a focus on the present.

Sensibly rationalizing our interactions in this fashion offers a clear framework from which to make sense of the often confusing nature of clinical work. Nevertheless, the reasonableness of this approach is periodically challenged where events transpiring within the treatment seem too unusual as to be adequately explained by it. As relational analyst Anthony Bass (2001, p. 688) writes: "Such moments, reflecting deep and sometimes mystifying points of connection and receptivity, have always been part of the experience of being an analyst." Nevertheless, psychoanalysts working outside the Jungian purview have generally not seen a need to pay more direct attention to these moments or examine how they might challenge and/or supplement existing theoretical models. Jungians would of course often tend to understand these moments in terms of synchronicity, though the gains in doing so are perhaps limited owing to Jung himself never explicitly integrating his ideas about synchronicity into his thinking about clinical practice. This is suggestive both of how much the relational psychoanalytic literature has to offer for Jungians, and of how much the Jungian literature has to offer for relational psychoanalysts.

Examining the ways in which enacted process unfolds outside the treatment draws attention to the need that psychoanalytic thinking about enactment be supplemented by Jungian thinking about synchronicity and the collective unconscious. In the controlled environment of the clinical setting the idea of mutual inducement can readily be invoked to ward off the threat of mystification—it is assumed that patient and clinician are constantly influencing each other in ways that are unconscious (hence potentially mystifying) but that this influence occurs via concrete behaviors wherein the participants impact each other causally (thus orchestrating the enacted dimension of the treatment). This line of thinking is no longer sufficient, however, where more explicitly synchronistic (i.e. acausal) moments of enactment occur under circumstances such as:

- between individuals who didn't have a prior relationship
- between individuals who have not been in recent contact
- between individuals and the animal world
- between individuals and events transpiring in the material environment

First Example

Michael, a fashion label owner approaching retirement age, admonished himself for what he considered his childish need for the approval of others. At present, this need was reflected most centrally in his relationship with his husband, Phillipe. Michael described Phillipe as ardently committed to his work as a fashion photographer. The two had met some 20 years previously when Michael hired Phillipe as an assistant. In the years that followed, however, the business had increasingly come to emphasize Phillipe's personal vision. Michael credited Phillipe as being "more creative" than him. Through our initial conversation it became apparent that Phillipe's approach to his work was obsessive, and that Michael's life was largely devoted to enabling Phillipe to function in his compulsions without these challenges becoming an obstacle to their daily living. Phillipe's attention to the immediate needs of work rendered him entirely unable to attend to the future. I had the image of Michael working tirelessly and subserviently to put enough road in front of them to prevent an accident. With the need to retire becoming more pressing, however, the status quo was becoming more difficult for Michael to maintain. No longer as physically fit as he once had been, keeping up with Phillipe's work demands seemed less and less viable. This became all the more apparent when Michael suffered a heart scare and was advised by his doctor to make lifestyle changes.

Significant context for this state of affairs could be discerned in Michael's youth. An only child, Michael received more care from his mother than he now felt was appropriate. He considered himself "spoiled" by his mother's unwaning attention. This perspective was supported in childhood by both of his parents: his mother would joke about the guilty pleasure she took in lavishing attention on her "little prince," while his father looked upon this indulgence disdainfully yet from an apparently uninvolved distance. Michael felt that his father considered him effeminate and pretentious. His father drank heavily and spent a lot of time in bars. Michael felt that there was an explicit alliance between himself and his mother which had been successful in its unspoken intention of distancing them both from his father.

When questioned about the nature of the indulgences he had been allowed as a boy, Michael shared memories of being taken by his mother to go clothes shopping and being dressed-up in the latest fashions. He considered himself fortunate in having enjoyed such a close relationship with his mother, for he had been prone to ill health and was frequently homebound—at his mother's insistence he was often shielded from the more strenuous demands of boyhood. Absences from school led to his being placed on academic probation.

Prompted by a distaste for what he considered his immature and fearful nature, despite his ill health, at a certain point in his teens Michael made a determined effort to participate more meaningfully in school life. He made concerted efforts to keep up with his peers, his grades improved significantly, and he was accepted to study at a respected university located several hundred miles from the family home. Not long after Michael left for the university, his mother began to encounter significant health issues of her own. She was subsequently diagnosed with cancer, and her health continued to decline over the course of Michael's studies. Less than two weeks after Michael completed his undergraduate studies, his mother died. With this loss Michael reported having felt a great pressure to "grow up" and enter adult life.

I drew attention to the inverse-correlation between Michael's health and that of his mother. Michael denied having previously noticed this connection himself. I suggested that it might be possible that this correlation hadn't registered consciously because of how painful it was. I also suggested that this might offer some sense of why the transition into retirement posed such a challenge: his efforts to support Phillipe in his obsessive functioning paralleled the supportive role he had played to his mother in childhood, while the looming threat of retirement had unconsciously constellated the trauma of his mother's death in relationship to the moment he had left home. This possibility was entertained by Michael with speculative interest, but didn't seem particularly impactful. Nevertheless, in the months that followed Michael became increasingly aware of the anger he felt towards Phillipe in relationship to the one-sidedness of their relationship. Attempts to verbalize his frustration were not well-received, further underscoring the basis for Michael's sense of discontent. Things came to a head when an unexpected opportunity arose to sell the business. Phillipe refused to entertain the possibility, but despite considerable resistance Michael insisted that the offer be given serious consideration.

On the day he was to enter formal negotiations to explore the possibility of selling, Michael received news that his former lover, Raul, had died in a plane crash. This news was met by Michael with profound grief and an overwhelming sense of guilt. Michael had been coupled with Raul for the best part of a decade, for much of which time the relationship had existed in a state of considerable uncertainty. Raul had been passionately committed to the relationship and had hoped that they would be able to adopt children. Michael didn't share these feelings, and was concerned by the sense of reliance he had developed on Raul to maintain social ties. Despite this, he had remained with Raul as an apparent consequence of his inability to be a disappointment to others.

News of Raul's death caused Michael to be flooded with guilt at the ways in which he thought of himself as having harmed Raul as a consequence of his inability to commit. This moment thus offered the emotional basis from which we were able to revisit the impact of his mother's death. It was now possible to draw a meaningful parallel between the ways in which his mother, Raul, and Phillipe each in their own way had refused to acknowledge the existence of Michael's own needs and experiences. Critical in bringing about this change was the happenstance timing of Raul's passing. In having occurred precisely at the point of emotional crisis in Michael's relationship with Phillipe, the timing of this event enabled the emotional Kairos out of which a meaningful change in participation could be realized.

The Role of Synchronicity

From an additive frame of reference (i.e. the patient's dynamics plus the analyst's), enactment is considered to be the effect of the patient and therapist joining in an unconscious performance that is reflective of their respective past experiences. While this performance is a shared creation, it is a creation that emerges from the unconscious contribution of the patient plus the unconscious contribution of the analyst. More constructive approaches to enactment, however, suggest the value of focusing on the primacy of the relational field as a whole greater than the sum of its apparent parts. But a field approach to practice must rest upon an appropriate model of reality. It is inconsistent to adopt a field approach to clinical interaction while one's underlying worldview still relies on a conception of the psyche that is reducible to the interaction of two discrete material entities existing only in physical space (see Brown, 2018b).

For Muslim mystic and philosopher Ibn al-'Arabī (1165–1240), to take material reality as the final ground of truth is a fundamental error that robs life of transcendence. The external world as we experience it is a product of the personal imagination which itself operates within the more fundamental domain of the imaginal. The oneiric nature of reality is reflected in the idea that whether an image is given inwardly or outwardly, it always expresses something other than itself and thus requires *ta'wil* (interpretation). As Izutsu (1983, p. 9) explains:

> We ordinarily admit without hesitation that a prophet perceives through and beyond his visions something ineffable, something of the true figure of the Absolute. In truth, however, not only such uncommon visions are symbolic "dreams" for a prophet. To his mind everything he sees, everything with which he is in contact even in daily life is liable to assume a symbolic character … The formal difference between the state of sleep (in which he sees things by the faculty of his imagination) and the state of wakefulness (in which he perceives things by his senses) is kept intact, yet in both states the things perceived are equally symbols.

The previous example reflects an attempt to illustrate the manner in which enacted process often depends upon a coincidence occurring between the inner life of the individual and events in the external world. While the relationship between Michael and Phillipe can potentially be understood in terms of mutual inducement, the crucial timing of Raul's death might give pause to wonder if a wider principle is at work. The notion of a meaningful coincidence between the individual and their world evokes what Jung (1952) intends by synchronicity. Jung's most often cited case of a clinical synchronicity is given with the scarab beetle incident.[2] This famous example can be understood in terms of a transpersonal conception of enactment (i.e. one that is not reducible to an additive understanding); in this instance, an enactment that proved to be generative (see Chapter 1 for a related discussion). Cambray (2019, p. 332) associates the unconscious connection between individuals with the occurrence of synchronistic phenomena in the analytic relationship. However, it should be noted that Jung himself did not articulate an equivalent notion to that of enactment. While enactment concerns the question of a coincidence between subjects in their unconscious relatedness, the emphasis with Jung's explication of synchronicity lies with a broader correspondence between psyche and matter. Jung's explicit theoretical elaboration of the synchronicity principle was in fact relatively limited, and he did little to examine this idea in relationship to the function of clinical work or the nature of interpersonal relatedness.[3] His focus was on positing this idea speculatively in terms of the latest developments in quantum physics.

Progoff (1973) points out that in seeking to establish synchronicity as a general scientific principle, Jung's work tends to foreground the more striking examples of synchronicity. This is understandable given that his initial concern was for having this phenomenon simply be understood and accepted as posing a legitimate question for science. However, Progoff, who knew Jung personally, contends that this emphasis is misleading, and that synchronicity was intended to be understood as a governing principle that substantially shapes our daily experience. This position is also supported by another close collaborator of Jung's, Marie-Louise von Franz:

> At first sight, "mirrorings" of psyche and matter that have the same meaning can be empirically established only in the relatively rare and irregularly occurring synchronistic events. It seems likely to me, however, that Jung's observation that the reconstruction of psychic processes in the microphysical world probably occurs as continuously as the psyche perceives the external world is to be understood in the sense that this mirror-relation exists *continuously* in the deeper layers of the unconscious but that we become aware of it only in certain exceptional situations in which synchronistic phenomena become observable. That would mean that in the deepest layer of the unconscious the psyche "knows" itself in the mirror of the cosmic world and that matter "knows" itself in the mirror of the objective psyche, but this "knowledge" is "absolute" in the sense that for our ego it is almost completely consciousness-transcending. Only in those rare moments when we are impressed by synchronistic phenomena do we become conscious of fragments or points of the mirror-relation.
>
> (von Franz, 1980, pp. 194–5)

The notion of enactment helps ground synchronicity as it manifests in a more subtle sense as a constant factor mediating our relatedness to the world. Meanwhile, in order to gain a more adequate picture of how enactment functions (i.e. inclusive of the transpersonal dimension), it is helpful if we supplement our existing thinking about this phenomenon with Jung's more abstract ideas about synchronicity. Doing so better allows us to understand the uncanny elements of enacted process reflected not only in the specificity of fit between patient and analyst, but also in terms of material events transpiring both inside and outside the treatment.

Second Example[4]

Yao, a Chinese-American man in his early twenties, had been hospitalized in a psychiatric inpatient unit owing to a persistent state of panic consequent upon his belief that the Chinese authorities had a hit out on him. He believed that he had the power to control governments, and that he was personally responsible for the US government shutdown of early 2019 which was taking place at the time of his hospitalization. Yao's family had moved to the United States when he was a child. He described himself as a "refugee," though records indicated otherwise. His family reported that they had kicked him out of the home owing to his unwillingness to stop smoking marijuana, which they considered to be the cause of his psychosis. Three days after Yao was admitted to the hospital, Brian, a US-born man of Northern European descent in his late fifties, was hospitalized to the same unit. At intake, Brian identified himself as a Chinese hitman who was feeling panicked by his homicidal ideation. Despite his rather imposing appearance, Brian's presentation was good-natured and gentle. Brian stated that he was a regular user of hallucinogenic substances, thus causing staff to question whether his psychotic presentation was merely consequent upon substance use. However, Brian's drug test came back negative. Brian expressed his wish to work with Chinese clinicians who he believed would be better able to understand him, and was disappointed when he was told that there were no Chinese clinicians working on the ward. Despite the startling coincidence between the presentation of these two patients, the bewildered hospital staff's main concern was to keep the two men apart out of a fear that their meeting might result in violence.

That Yao would experience himself as a refugee suggests a sense of being threatened from within the family, as does the fear of being executed by a Chinese operative. In Yao's world, the notion of *government* would appear to stand both for his family, and for the structure of his own personality. To claim responsibility for the government shutdown is thus both to assume responsibility for his family rejecting him, and for his own state of psychosis. Smoking marijuana provided an apparent way out of the family, but while this act draws attention to the family system's hostility (kicking him out leading to his being assigned refugee status) it simultaneously denies it by making "the fault" his own (choosing to smoke and being responsible for the "shutdown"). Meanwhile, Brian considers himself to be a dangerous and drug-addled hitman, yet he had willingly admitted himself to the hospital out of concern for hurting others. We might speculate that Brian's identification with the role of a Chinese hitman reflects a sense of himself as an outsider (from a foreign culture) and of his feeling personally responsible for terminating his relationship with others (a hitman). Yao and Brian both identify themselves as powerful and dangerous men, yet they both voluntarily had themselves hospitalized owing to a concern about their powerlessness—Yao to prevent the Chinese government from taking his life, and Brian from being able to resist his murderous nature.

What would the possible enactive consequences be of these two individuals encountering each other? Given the parallel concerns of the two men, we might speculate that their meeting could well be of considerable therapeutic benefit—assuming we endorse an idea that meaningful coincidence exists and has a teleological purpose. It doesn't seem farfetched to assume that Brian's wish to connect with Chinese people (who he feels understand him better) could readily lead to his striking up a friendly relationship with Yao. For Yao, we might imagine the older Brian symbolizing a threatening image of authority (the very hitman he had been expecting) who might nevertheless come to be rendered more relatable. Equally, for Brian, Yao might suggest himself as a relatable embodiment of Brian's own vulnerability and of the tendency he takes to assume responsibility for his own isolation. This would reflect a potential challenge to his sense of himself as ruthlessly self-interested (murderous). However, in rationalistic flight from the craziness of the coincidence itself, the hospital staff *fear violence* and, in denial of the violence perpetrated by the psychiatric system, seek to prevent the two patients from ever meeting. In this way, the imposed order of the hospital system enactively recapitulates the imposed order that both individual's experience in terms of a belief in their own destructiveness.

Possibilities for Integration

A Jungian approach to enactment offers a framework for integration not only between analytical psychology and relational psychoanalysis, but also between relational and post-Bionian field theories. The "oneiric paradigm" associated with contemporary Bionian practice, and in particular with the work of Antonino Ferro, suggests that we should always listen to the patient as though they were relating a dream. It is important to note, however, that for Ferro it is the patient's *narrative* which is to be heard as a dream, not the actuality. This approach nevertheless has the advantage of training clinical attention on the personal meanings constantly being reflected in the patient's discourse. An intrapsychic approach of this kind fosters an ear for metaphor and insists that the clinician should always be wary of falling into literalism.

Despite these advantages, relational thinking poses broad challenges to the oneiric outlook. Donnel Stern (2015) draws our attention to the fashion in which an exclusive emphasis on the intrapsychic doesn't do enough to account for the impact of the external world—an essential element of which would include the impact of the analyst. While Ferro and other post-Bionian analysts do acknowledge the way in which the analytic field is shaped by both participants, their understanding of the analyst's involvement is that it is fundamentally responsive to the patient's lead. It is believed that the analyst is able to function without imposing their own subjectivity on the treatment.

Rather, the analyst's subjectivity optimally serves only in its function vis-à-vis the container-contained relationship.

From a relational perspective, Stern argues convincingly that Ferro has not done enough to immunize his approach such as to ensure that his clinical influence will be personally disinterested. In effect, the post-Bionian approach still suffers from one of the major deficiencies associated with classical Freudian thinking in that it is assumed that self-reflection on the part of the analyst can largely mitigate for the emergence of the analyst's own unconscious dynamics in the treatment. The post-Bionian outlook claims that it is possible to step outside of the intrapsychic field (constituted by the container–contained relationship) in order to self-supervise. As Katz (2017, p. 104) puts it, the analyst in this model "is viewed as able to cross a boundary in order to move back and forth from being immersed in the analytic dreaming to interacting with it. Being outside is like having awakened from the dream."

From a Jungian perspective it might be argued that the limitation of Ferro's outlook is not in approaching the reported events of a patient's life as always expressive of psychic reality, but in constraining the basis of this expressiveness purely in terms of a narrative offered in relationship to the analyst functioning as container/interpreter of the patient's experience. In this light it is merely the contextual reporting of a given event which is considered psychically expressive and not the event itself. A Jungian approach to enactment radically challenges the distinction between the psyche and a world in some sense external to it, thus facilitating a way of listening which searches for a possible meaning in the events themselves. Relationalists have similarly sought to complexify and problematize hard distinctions between the intrapsychic and the interpersonal. However, this uncertainty is an epistemological one concerning the limits of knowing. Broadly speaking, relational thinking stops short of formalizing this uncertainty as a claim about the nature of reality itself. An implicit ontological distinction between inner and outer worlds remains unchallenged. Consequently, the value of the post-Bionian ear for metaphor may sometimes be threatened—this being reflected wherever the external world is considered only as a cause and not in any sense *expressive* of psychic life.

Summary

Since the psychoanalytic notion of enactment rose to prominence more than 30 years ago, the phenomenon thus addressed has undergone extensive theoretical elaboration. Early thinking tended to foreground the idea of discrete enactments which had to be consciously identified in order to prevent disruption to the treatment. Significant developments have been reflected in the broadening of this concept to acknowledge enactment as an ongoing feature of all human relations and, more recently, in exploring the ways in which enactment may often be considered creative. Building on these claims, I have argued that the causal explanation of "mutual inducement" is insufficient.

Drawing from Jung's ideas about synchronicity I have adopted the notion of meaningful coincidence to offer a Jungian conception of enactment. I suggest that this modified conception of enactment offers a useful corrective to the typological one-sidedness implied by Jung's ideas about projection.

Notes

1 Focusing on our perception of events external to the treatment (based, that is, on the patient's reports of them) always raises the danger of being considered psychologically naive. However, such claims tend to hinge on a certain kind of literalism which is perhaps itself more problematic. Nonetheless, the clinical intent not to assume a naively authoritative stance on events occurring outside the relationship with the analyst is an important one. This helps explain why many relational writers may perhaps prioritize the implicit/enacted dimension of the analytic relationship as the decisive factor in bringing about change. By focusing too much on relationships outside of the treatment we are possibly in danger of forfeiting a recognition of the relationality of the treatment itself. However well founded this kind of caution might be, however, it seems reasonable to suppose that even a deeply impactful analysis can only be treated as one significant transformative factor in the person's life, and that events outside the consultation room may often be a good deal more significant in this respect than what occurs during session. Failure to account for this is liable to substantially distort our theorizing.

2 "My example concerns a young woman patient who, in spite of efforts made on both sides, proved to be psychologically inaccessible. The difficulty lay in the fact that she always knew better about everything. Her excellent education had provided her with a weapon ideally suited to this purpose, namely a highly polished Cartesian rationalism with an impeccably "geometrical" idea of reality. After several fruitless attempts to sweeten her rationalism with a somewhat more human understanding, I had to confine myself to the hope that something unexpected and irrational would turn up, something that would burst the intellectual retort into which she had sealed herself. Well, I was sitting opposite her one day, with my back to the window, listening to her flow of rhetoric. She had an impressive dream the night before, in which someone had given her a golden scarab – a costly piece of jewelry. While she was still telling me this dream, I heard something behind me gently tapping on the window. I turned round and saw that it was a fairly large flying insect that was knocking against the window-pane from outside in the obvious effort to get into the dark room. This seemed to me very strange. I opened the window immediately and caught the insect in the air as it flew in. It was a scarabaeid beetle, or common rose-chafer (*Cetonia aurata*), whose gold-green color most nearly resembles that of a golden scarab. I handed the beetle to my patient with the words, "Here is your scarab." This experience punctured the desired hole in her rationalism and broke the ice of her intellectual resistance. The treatment could now be continued with satisfactory results." (Jung, 1952, para. 982)

3 The extent to which Jung's clinical thinking sometimes coincides with the psychoanalytic ideas I am here seeking to challenge is reflected in the following quote: "The patient, by bringing an unconscious content to bear upon the doctor, constellates the corresponding unconscious material in him, owing to the inductive effect which always emanates from projections in greater or lesser degree. Doctor and patient thus find themselves in a relationship founded on mutual unconsciousness." (Jung, 1946, para. 364) Jung here relies on the idea of inducement thus positing the relational field as a co-creation of two individuals rather than as an ontological reality which itself establishes the basis for relationship.

4 This example was originally discussed in my book *Groundwork for a Transpersonal Psychoanalysis* (Brown, 2020, and the material is reproduced here with permission of the publisher. Further examples and discussion are offered in this work. Also see Brown (2018a) and Brown & Brown (2021).

References

Atlas, G., & Aron, L. (2018). *Dramatic Dialogue: Contemporary Clinical Practice.* Routledge.

Bass, A. (2001). It takes one to know one; or, whose unconscious is it anyway? *Psychoanalytic Dialogues,* 11(5), 683–702.

Brooke, R. (1991). *Jung and Phenomenology.* Routledge.

Brown, R. S. (2014). Evolving attitudes. *International Journal of Jungian Studies,* 6(3), 243–253.

Brown, R. S. (2017). *Psychoanalysis Beyond the End of Metaphysics: Thinking Towards the Post-Relational.* Routledge.

Brown, R. S. (2018a). Imaginal action: towards a Jungian conception of enactment, and an extraverted counterpart to active imagination. *Journal of Analytical Psychology,* 63 (2), 186–206.

Brown, R. S. (2018b). *Re-Encountering Jung: Analytical Psychology and Contemporary Psychoanalysis.* Routledge.

Brown, R. S. (2020). *Groundwork for a Transpersonal Psychoanalysis: Spirituality, Relationship, and Participation.* Routledge.

Brown, R. S., & Brown, M. (2021). Transpersonal enactments and the teleology of paranoia. In M. Brown & R. S. Brown (eds.). *Emancipatory Perspectives on Madness: Psychological, Social, and Spiritual Dimensions,* 35–49. Routledge.

Buirski, P. (2005). *Practicing Intersubjectively.* Jason Aronson.

Cambray, J. (2019). The Red Book today: from novelty to innovation - not art but nature. In M. Stein & T. Arzt (eds.), *Jung's Red Book for Our Time (vol. 3): Searching for Soul Under Postmodern Conditions.* Chiron.

Freud, S. (1914). Remembering, repeating and working-through (further recommendations on the technique of psychoanalysis II). In *The Standard Edition of the Complete Psychological Works of Sigmund Freud, Vol. 12,* 145–156.

Izutsu, T. (1983). *Sufism & Taoism: A Comparative Study of Key Philosophical Concepts.* University of California Press.

Jung, C.G. (1946). The psychology of the transference. In C. G. Jung, *Collected Works,* 353–537. Princeton University Press.

Jung, C.G. (1952). Synchronicity: an acausal connecting principle. In C. G. Jung, *Collected Works,* 417–531. Princeton University Press.

Jung, C. G. (1988). *Nietzsche's "Zarathustra": Notes of the Seminar Given in 1934–1939 by C. G. Jung, Vols.* 1 & 2. (J. L. Jarrett, Ed.). Princeton University Press.

Katz, S. M. (2017). *Contemporary Psychoanalytic Field Theory: Stories, Dreams, and Metaphor.* Routledge.

Mitchell, S. A. (1984). Object relations theories and the developmental tilt. *Contemporary Psychoanalsis,* 20, 473–499.

Progoff, I. (1973). *Jung, Synchronicity, and Human Destiny.* Julian Press.

Saban, M. (2019). *'Two Soul Alas': Jung's Two Personalities and the Making of Analytical Psychology.* Chiron Press.

Searles, H. F. (1975). Patient as therapist to his analyst. In H. F. Searles, *Countertransference and Related Subjects: Selected Papers*, 380–459. International Universities Press.

Stern, D. B. (2015). *Relational Freedom: Emergent Properties of the Interpersonal Field*. Routledge.

Stolorow R. D., & Atwood G. E. (1992). *Contexts of Being: The Intersubjective Foundations of Psychological Life*. Analytic Press.

von Franz, M.-L. (1980). *Projection and Re-collection in Jungian Psychology: Reflections of the Soul*. (W. H. Kennedy, Trans.). Open Court Publishing Company.

Wachtel, P. L. (2008). *Relational Theory and the Practice of Psychotherapy*. The Guildford Press.

Wachtel, P. L. (2017). The relationality of everyday life: the unfinished journey of relational psychoanalysis. *Psychoanalytic Dialogues*, 27(5), 503–521.

Chapter 4

Soul in the World

Symbolic Culture as the Medium for Psyche[1]

Warren Colman

The idea of the *anima mundi* or world-soul is an attractive notion with a long history. In its original incarnation in Plato's *Timaeus* it directly refers to the animation of the world, universe or cosmos. Plato conceives of the world as a living being, endowed with soul and intelligence, encompassing all the living creatures within it (2008, 30b, 30d). This is a vision rooted in a cultural world where science and myth had not yet been differentiated so there was no contradiction between an animistic vision of the physical world and a demonstration of its nature in terms of mathematical geometry. The relation between soul and body also carried ethical implications. Plato considered that the aim of life was to recover the perfect revolutions of the soul from the perturbations caused by the chaos of the senses and this was linked to a belief in reincarnation in a more or less perfect bodily form, a view that nevertheless held humans and other animals to be ontologically equivalent by virtue of their common possession of a soul (Carpenter, 2008). There are thus many linkages between Plato's thought and similar animistic beliefs still found in many cultures all over the world.

Yet there is also a crack in Plato's world that has grown into the great divide between body and soul, matter and spirit that has rent the modern world in two – a split that Jung laboured to heal in the world and himself throughout his life and work. It is not so much that Plato conceives of body and soul as separate, for many animistic cultures have beliefs about the circulation of souls through various cosmic forms; it is rather that Plato sets up a clear hierarchy between the two, made most apparent in *The Symposium*, where he contrasts the love of absolute, divine beauty with the grossly inferior love of physical beauty which he describes as 'a mass of perishable rubbish' (Plato, 1951, 212).

This notion of the inferiority of the body and the physical world came to play an increasingly dominant role in the Christian world, exemplified by St. Paul's view that 'the desires of the flesh are against the Spirit and the desires of the Spirit against the flesh' (Galatians 5: 16–17), a much more extreme conflict than we find in Plato. The more that soul is seen as the true and only source of life, the more the material world comes to be seen as devoid of life

DOI: 10.4324/9781003429142-4

and divorced from spirit. This trend became clearly apparent in the scientific revolution of the 17th century and found its philosophical expression in the work of Descartes. Descartes' explicit intention was to rid philosophy of the old Aristotelean (and latterly Christian) idea of things in the world having the teleological qualities of soul (Descartes, 2009, p. 163) The aim of this deanimation was to clear the way for science to explore the world in terms of purely physical mechanisms. Since the body is part of the physical world, then surely it too must be purely mechanical, thus giving rise to the problem of how mind and brain are connected. Over the past two centuries, this trend has gone even further: not only have we come to see the mind as separated off from the material world but we have come to doubt whether the mind has any kind of soul at all or is merely an expression of the physical activity of the brain.

The scientific method developed in the 17th century has been spectacularly successful as a means of understanding the natural world and harnessing its forces for industrial and technological transformation. Yet this has come at a high price, often described in terms of the desacralisation and pillaging of the natural world, together with the alienation, isolation, and loss of meaning that characterise Western societies.

Esse in Anima—Jung's Solution to the Isolated Cartesian Mind

Jung tried to reconnect the isolated modern human psyche to the world soul. Despite this, his attitude towards the severance of mind from world was ambivalent and contradictory, reflecting the split in himself between Number 1 and Number 2 personalities. In his Number 2 personality, Jung felt identified with 'the spirit of the depths' (Jung, 2009, p. 229). In this aspect, Jung experienced for himself the oneness of the world with the living soul and many of his major concepts reflect this, especially the self, the psyche, the unconscious and latterly the archetypes. All these concepts implicitly transcend the boundaries of the individual mind and include aspects that unite our personal lives with something far greater, for which the *anima mundi* and the *unus mundus* are both symbolic expressions. Yet the revolutionary transformations brought about by Jung's 'confrontation with the unconscious' did not dispel the firmly held beliefs of his Number 1 personality, rooted in the 'spirit of the times' (Jung, 2009, p. 229) Jung was not willing to give up his scientific convictions to become a mystic or prophet but, throughout his life, sought to reconcile the one with the other.

These opposing tendencies can be seen quite clearly in the following quotation:

> The development of Western philosophy during the last two centuries has succeeded in isolating the mind in its own sphere and in severing it from its primordial oneness with the universe. Man himself has ceased to be the microcosm and eidolon of the cosmos, and his 'anima' is no longer the consubstantial scintilla, spark of the *Anima mundi*, World Soul.
>
> (Jung, 1939, para. 759)

On the surface, it appears as if Jung is lamenting this trend and eulogising the lost union with the anima. Yet, if we read further, it becomes apparent that Jung not only accepts the Cartesian divide between mind and world but regards it as a positive progression. This is most apparent in his view that pre-Cartesian ways of being in the world were the result of 'projections' that hark back to a more primitive condition that modern man has now left behind:

> If we accept the restrictions imposed upon the capacity of our mind ... we bid farewell to that miraculous world in which mind-created things and beings move and live. This is the world of the primitive, where even inanimate objects are endowed with a living, healing, magic power, through which they participate in us and we in them. Sooner or later we had to understand that their potency was really ours, and that their significance was our projection.
>
> (Jung, 1939, para. 761)

Elsewhere he writes 'through the withdrawal of projections, conscious knowledge slowly developed' (Jung, 1938, para. 140) and expresses the view 'that there is, in a certain sense, nothing that is directly experienced except the mind itself' (Jung, 1926, para. 623). Thus he accepts without question the view that 'cognition is a mental faculty and, if carried beyond the human plane, a projection' (Jung, 1939, para. 765) and that man is therefore 'shut up inside his mind and cannot step beyond it' (Jung, 1939, para. 765). Jung derived most of this from Kant's rejection of transcendent knowledge and his strictures on the fundamental unknowability of the 'thing in itself'. Yet the image of being 'shut up inside his mind' is also a perfect representation for Descartes' 'cogito ergo sum', in which only the contents of his own thinking mind can be guaranteed as real. Jung's approach is therefore to render unto Kant and Descartes what is due to Kant and Descartes but then to seek a way of nevertheless rendering unto God what is due to God – and to the *anima mundi*.

His solution is an ingenious one: to the conflict between *esse in intellectu* (being in the mind) and *esse in re* (being in actuality), Jung proposes a third possibility, *esse in anima* (being in soul), and he makes this the overarching reality that incorporates the other two (Jung, 1921, paras. 66, 77). Jung's ploy here is to take the notion of psyche as the primary datum, the only thing which we can directly know, and then suggest that since both the phenomenal and noumenal worlds are experienced psychically, they can be interpreted as functions of the psyche. Furthermore, since what is most important in the psyche is not mere consciousness but the vast untapped resources of the unconscious and especially the archetypes, it is the archetypes that become the real powerhouse, not only of psychic life but of the world as a whole. The entirety of world history and ultimately the cosmos itself can be seen as the manifestation of the archetypes. But rather than this being seen philosophically, as in Plato's Ideal Forms or religiously as in the Christian notion of God's will, it can now be demonstrated psychologically, and therefore scientifically.

The origins of this ingenious solution lie in Jung's encounter with the god Izdubar, reported in *The Red Book*. Izdubar, the old God of the East, cannot survive the encounter with modern science from the West which threatens to kill him off altogether in Neitzschian style. So Jung offers him a way out—he puts the god in his pocket and preserves him as a psychic image, a fantasy. Yet this fantasy, it turns out, is mightier than anything else because it is the psyche that *creates* reality. As he formulated it in 'Psychological Types':

> What indeed is reality if it is not a reality in ourselves, an *esse in anima*? Living reality is the product neither of the actual objective behaviour of things nor of the formulated idea exclusively, but rather of the combination of both in the living psychological process, through *esse in anima* ... *The psyche creates reality every day.* The only expression I can use for this activity is *fantasy.*
>
> (Jung, 1921, paras. 77–78)

By this means, Jung is able to use the reality of the psyche as a trump card with which to put not only Izdubar in his pocket but the science and philosophy that threatened to kill him off. Psychological explanations trump philosophical ones by revealing their underlying archetypal origins. Yet despite this ingenious solution, Jung was still unable to reconcile the divide between spirit and matter, body and soul that preoccupies his later work on synchronicity, the psychoid, and the attempt to find a common ground between atomic physics and archetypal psychology.

In my view, these difficulties were because Jung made the wrong call in accepting the Kantian/Cartesian limitations on the mind as 'shut up in its own sphere', isolated from the living world in which we actually participate all the time. It is this disconnect in Jungian psychology itself that results in frequent attempts to interpret world events as the expression of archetypal forces, as if the real forces at work in our collective lives are not geography, climate, competition for resources and social and political conflict but 'the great mother', 'the trickster', 'the shadow' or 'the anima'. To my mind, this not only fails to address the complex interrelation between states of mind and the state of the social world but reduces the latter to a kind of ghost-life as if it is merely a screen for psychic projections.

An example of this can be found in Jung's 1936 essay where he interprets events in Nazi Germany as the re-awakening of Wotan in the German psyche. It is not difficult to see that the catastrophic economic conditions in Weimar Germany, together with the humiliating shock of defeat in the First World War, would have evoked states of fear, confusion, rage and impotence to which Nazi ideology appeared to offer a radical solution. Wotan may be a very useful metaphor for this that roots the specific features of National Socialism in German history and the symbols of German culture. But Jung goes much further than this to suggest that Wotan is 'a fundamental attribute of the German psyche' (1936, para. 389) whose 'unfathomable depths ... explain more of National Socialism than [economic, political and psychological factors] put together' (1936, para. 385). Jung takes his own metaphor as a causal explanation, as if it is not the aftermath of the First World War that has created these social conditions, but that history itself is to be understood as the working out of archetypal forces, an argument pursued on a grand scale in *Aion*.

In my view, if we are to appreciate how the soul lives in the world, we need first to see how living in the world creates the soul. To do so, we need to tackle the Cartesian worldview at its roots, challenging the separation between mind and world in favour of an approach that relocates the mind in embodied action in the world.

Embodiment, Practice and the Extended Mind

The roots of this alternative view go back to Aristotle's very different view of the relation between body and soul. For Aristotle, the soul cannot exist without the body so it makes no sense to think of them as separate entities.[2] As Richard Swinburne explains:

> Aristotle thought of the soul simply as ... a way of behaving and thinking: a human having a soul just is the human behaving and thinking in certain characteristic human ways. And just as there cannot be a dance without people dancing, so there cannot be ways of behaving without embodied humans to behave in those ways.
>
> (Swinburne, 2000, pp. 851–852)

The soul is simply the actuality of a living being, it is what makes them the kind of thing they are. This leads to a strong emphasis on practical action and behaviour in Aristotle's thought – concepts like *phronesis*, the practical wisdom garnered by experience, and *techne*, the practical action of making and doing, as opposed to the disinterested understanding of *episteme*.

Aristotle's view of embodied souls engaged in practical action is the philosophical ancestor of modern phenomenological approaches that see cognition as inherently tied to the material world, arising in and through our engagement with things and other people. Cognition is therefore best understood, as 'the exercise of skilful know-how in situated and embodied action' (Thompson, 2007, p. 11). We learn about the world as it presents itself to us and acts upon us. This means that even the material world of supposedly inanimate matter has agency in the cognitive process.

Consider, for example, the making of stone tools. Almost two million years ago, an early hominin species known as *Homo erectus* began making stone tools in a characteristic teardrop shape known as Acheulean axes. These axes remained in use until a mere 60,000 years ago which makes them arguably the most important technological advance of all time. Many of these tools are so pleasing to the eye (and hand) that it seems as if they must have been made with conscious intention by people with a well-developed aesthetic sensibility. Yet it is more likely that their shape and form were determined by the practical engagement of the knapping process – the striking of flakes from cores. Cognitive archaeologist Lambros Malafouris argues that knapping activity does not arise 'within' the mind and is then enacted – it is the actual practice of knapping that shapes the knapper's intentions as he or she discovers what the stone itself requires.

> The best angles for flake removal are neither identified nor imagined in the knapper's head before the act ... they are embodied and therefore they must be discovered in action. ... The stone projects towards the knapper as much as the knapper projects toward the stone and together they delineate the cognitive map of what we may call an *extended intentional state*. The knapper first thinks *through* and *with* the stone before being able to think *about* the stone and hence about himself as a conscious and reflectively aware agent.
>
> (Malafouris, 2013, pp. 174, 176)

In this view, the stone itself is an active element in the cognitive process. This is an example of what philosopher Andy Clark has called the extended mind – the idea that the tools and technologies used by humans are not merely aids to cognition but are intrinsically part of the cognitive process (Clark & Chalmers, 1998). This can be illustrated in relation to the alchemical *opus*. Jung interprets this almost entirely in terms of projection. He assumes that what the alchemists saw in their retorts and vats were projections of their own psyche and that what they were 'really' engaged in transforming was themselves, a process of individuation. Yet this misses the point that the alchemical *opus* was essentially an embodied practice undertaken with material elements and objects. Their metaphorical accounts were inseparable from this practice just as soul is inseparable from the body in Aristotle's account. There is no way to sever the material activity with mercury, sulphur and lead from the symbolic meanings with which these materials were imbued; arguably, it may only have been through the practice that the symbolic meanings could be understood.

The mind is not, as Andy Clark puts it, bound by skin and skull but extends into the world. *A fortiori*, the mind is dependent on the world which it cognises to exist at all and especially, of course, the human body. So the only way we could ever 'build a human mind', the holy grail of artificial intelligence, would be to build a human body together with the species specific environment in which the human body functions. Already, then, we are long way from being 'shut up in the mind and unable to step beyond it'. Nor are we shut up in our bodies since our bodies are open to the world at every pore.

What confuses us as we reflect upon our self-reflective minds is our capacity to create virtual worlds in the space of our own imagination. I suspect that this is often what we mean when we say 'psyche'; it is certainly what is meant by terms such as the 'internal world' and its characteristic mode of fantasy. Yet imagination would not be possible without the symbols we use to imagine with and these depend on our engagement with an environment, especially the cultural environment of symbols in which all humans live. Symbols are the tools we use to think with and because we are able to use these tools 'in our minds' without apparent converse with the world of things and other people, we tend to believe that this activity is going on 'in our heads' and that the mind is therefore a separate thing from the world we inhabit. I now want to show why I consider this to be a mistaken illusion.

Shared Language, Distributed Cognition and Constitutive Symbols

Let me start with language. Here I am using the term symbol in its wider meaning as a representation of one thing by another in a conventionally agreed system of meanings. Other animals communicate by means of indicative signs such as the vervet monkey whose cry warns the troupe of an approaching predator. Human symbolic language is quite different from this because the symbols of language are, we might say, self-standing – they continue to exist and have meaning even in the absence of the things to which they refer (Deacon, 1997). 'Fire' means 'fire' whether there's a fire in the hotel or not, whereas a dog will soon cease to respond to the sound 'walk' if an actual walk fails to take place soon afterwards. For the dog, the word is only an indicator not a symbol. That is, the symbols of human language have a *virtual* existence and meaning which enable us to imagine a fire or a walk independently of the actual events.

Now for this to be the case, these meanings have to be shared. That is, language and the use of symbols generally is primarily a form of communication and therefore can only develop in the context of shared communication *between* people. Language relies on a pre-existing context of social co-operation and common ground within which speakers are able to recognise each other's intention to communicate and what they are likely to be communicating about (Tomasello, 2008). This kind of mutual co-operation is virtually unique amongst humans.[3] We also communicate not only for imperative reasons – what we want from others – but in order to share with each other and help each other. For example, young children spontaneously begin to point at around one year old, not only to ask for things but to declare their interest and pleasure and share that with others (Tomasello, 2008) Declarative pointing is also used in conjunction with language learning: a child may point out an object of delight and the parent will add the word 'Yes, it's a *bus!*' And on a later occasion the child will point and say to the parent 'Bus!' (Colman, 2016, p. 109).

Thus human language is a fundamentally social activity in which meanings are constructed and shared between people prior to their being a means of private thought. Without language, Descartes could never have formulated the thought that he was thinking. It is only through our communication with others that we come to know we exist at all. It would be more true to say 'I think, therefore we are' but it is even more the case that 'We are, therefore I think'.

This is true not only for language but for cognition more generally. Far from being a faculty of isolated minds, human cognition is distributed between agents acting together in shared endeavours. This has been extensively demonstrated by Edwin Hutchins, initially in relation to ships' navigators but subsequently in many other fields as well. In a modern elaboration of Aristotle's *techne,* Hutchins showed that the reasoning processes of navigators involved an interaction between embodied gestures, material objects (tools) and shared communications with colleagues working on a shared task (Hutchins, 1995).

From a different perspective, philosopher Shaun Gallagher (2012) has shown how cognition is distributed amongst social groups so that the individual mind is extended through participation with others. Social and cultural institutions such as educational, scientific and professional institutions, the legal system and religious organizations, all act as repositories of previously established cognitive information. Learning to think within the rules and procedures of these established institutions greatly enhances the cognitive resources available to individual actors who do not have to rely on creating their own knowledge *ab novo.* For example, 'legal judgments are not confined to individual brains, or even to the many brains that constitute a particular court. They emerge in the workings of a large and complex institution'. Gallagher concludes that 'human cognition relies not simply on localized brain processes in any particular individual ... but often on social processes that extend over long periods of time' (2012, p. 63).

Distributed cognition is a key feature of the adaptations responsible for human evolutionary success, based in the development of social co-operation and common ground. By encoding information in symbolic form, humans became able to pass on their learning from one generation to another. The development of brain capable of processing symbolic information is thus already sufficient to open up the possibility of social and psychological change without this requiring any further change to the genome, giving humans a unique adaptive capacity. As sociologist Norbert Elias says, 'Human beings are biologically capable of changing their manner of social life. By virtue of their evolutionary endowment they can develop socially'

(Elias, 2011, p. 52). So, for example, there is no need to postulate some kind of genetic modification to account for the develoment of painting, sculpture and increasingly complex tools in the Upper Palaeolithic period of around 40,000 years ago: the necessary biological changes would have arleady been in place from the time of the first early modern humans some 200,000 years ago. Symbols also enable us to develop psychologically by creating symbolic form and meaning for inchoate thought and feeling, especially the symbols of dream, art and myth whose meanings rely on potentially infinite metaphorical associations, giving them the necessary fluidity to express the complex nuances of our intangible psychic life (the world of soul and spirit).

Crucially, many symbols do not merely *represent* meanings but *constitute* them, bringing into being the realities they represent (Searle, 1995; Colman, 2015, pp. 529–532; Colman, 2016 pp. 151–168). Archaeologist Colin Renfrew provides a useful illustration of this point. The introduction of stone weights in Neolithic cultures created the *concept* of weight which could not exist without material symbols to represent it. Weight as a symbol of weight, as Renfrew puts it. Such concepts do not come out of our minds but, as Renfrew says, must first have been apprehended through physical experience – you could not make it up if you had not experienced it (Renfrew, 2008, p. 117). But the concept of weight only arises in a social context where measurement has become necessary. Thus the concept as idea comes after the fact of physical experience and the exigencies of embodied social living.

Now just as the physical property of heaviness exists prior to the concept of weight, there are certainly psychic qualities that exist prior to their symbolisation, mainly in the area of affect. Emotion is the way we register what is significant to us in our environment, primarily via attraction and avoidance. It is also a means of communication which we share with other animals. But human emotion is far more extensive and differentiated than that of any other animal and this, I suggest, is also the result of its symbolisation in a social context. Ritual has a key role to play here in the evocation, containment and management of powerful affects in the context of creating social meanings (Colman, 2016, pp. 251–257).

But by the same token this means that symbolic forms of culture such as ritual are as essential to knowing what we feel as language is essential to knowing what we think. Our specifically human emotional life has developed within a particular environment, the environment of human symbolic culture. Symbolic culture is the human *Umwelt*. So deeply is culture written into our emotional and psychological lives that we could not be human without it. Culture is our nature and our relation to the natural, 'more than human world' is cultural through and through.[4] Take away symbolic culture and we become, in Clifford Geertz' evocative phrase, 'formless monster[s] with neither sense of direction nor power of self-control, a chaos of spasmodic impulses and vague emotions' (Geertz, 1973, p. 99).

Effectively this means that symbols create the psyche, rather than the psyche creating symbols, albeit this occurs, as I have shown, via the processes of social and bodily engagement with the material world. In this reversed view, the soul is not as Plato believed, the 'senior partner' in the body/soul relationship and 'the place where belief and knowledge arise' (2008, 34c); rather the soul is a symbol that long post-dates our bodily engagement in the world and its existence depends on the systems of symbolic representation through which it could originally be conceived – please note the embodied metaphor here. This does not, of course, imply that the soul is 'not real', as if it is 'merely' a symbol. As I have explained, it is in the nature of constitutive symbols to create the realities they represent. In a sense, before we can have a soul (or a self) we have to be able to 'think a soul' and we can only do that within a socially generated system of collective representations.

Collective Representations and *Participation Mystique*

Such systems are the means by which social groups formulate and pass on their accumulated knowledge and understanding of the world. Here again, we can see how Jung demoted social reality in favour of the psyche as the primary datum (Segal, 2007). In Durkheim's original usage, collective representations referred to the symbolic systems by which a society represented itself, particularly in its ritual practices and beliefs. The term was taken up by Lévy-Bruhl (1910) to explain the quality of *participation mystique* that characterised what he thought of as 'pre-logical thinking'. Lévy-Bruhl argued that this was not simply an inferior version of modern rational thinking but something qualitatively different, due to the very different collective representations pertaining in 'native' societies, as they were then called. This included beliefs in a mystical unity between objects, animals and humans as well as animistic beliefs about the agency of so-called 'inanimate' elements of Nature. For Lévy-Bruhl, then, *participation mystique* refers to socially organized perceptions, practices and beliefs that are formulated and impressed on the mind in affectively charged conditions, notably ritual.

Jung took up these terms in a quite different way. In Jung's usage, both collective representations and *participation mystique* originate not in society but in the psyche. Collective representations become the archetypes of the collective unconscious and *participation mystique* becomes projection or, in more recent parlance, projective identification. Jung replaces the social group with 'the collective psyche' and thereby loses the sense of human participation in the group which is then reduced to 'unconsciousness'. He desocialises collective representations so that they become merely 'psychic contents' (Jung, 1921, para. 692). In this way, he severs the link between the psychic world and the social world and loses the most significant feature of Lévy-Bruhl's thought – the recognition that people think as they do not because they exist in a state of primitive unconsciousness but because they live in a different form of society in different environmental conditions and their thought is structured in different ways (Segal, 2007, p. 636).

However, despite this important insight, Lévy-Bruhl nevertheless maintained the prevalent view that people who thought in this way were 'primitive' and that *participation mystique* belonged to a 'lower' form of society that had been superseded by the 'higher type' of 19th-century Europe. In this way he showed himself to be just a much a creature of collective representations as the so-called primitives. For the upshot of Durkheim's analysis is that we are *all* subject to our collective representations and it is extremely difficult to think outside them. These collective symbolic forms are the matrix that shape and constrain our psychic sensibilities. They are the lens through which we experience the world and, as such, we are usually unaware of them – they are what we take for granted. So while we no longer accept that indigenous peoples are 'primitive', nor do we really understand how they think and why. Most of us find it exceedingly difficult to make sense of things like rain-making, spirit travel, shamanic practices or even, truth be told, synchronicity, which we prefer to re-interpret in more familiar psychological terms. Just as other cultures take for granted that dreams are a message from the ancestors or a journey into the realm of the spirits, we take for granted that they are psychological events that take place in our heads and are, at best, a message from the unconscious. *We* know that the mind exists in the head and is separate from the world around us, that the inorganic world is not a living world and that there is something called Nature from which we have become separated, a belief powerfully expressed in the ancient myth of our expulsion from the Garden of Eden, a collective representation *par excellence*. We also know that objects are made up of atoms, that the universe was created in a Big Bang 14 billion years ago and a whole host of other things we do not really understand in the slightest but accept virtually without question, like the Red Queen in *Alice Through the Looking-Glass* who believed six impossible things before breakfast. Above all, we accept that the scientific method is the guarantor of truth and we must either prove things within its terms or create an alternative enclave called 'religion' or 'the psyche' or, in my own term a few years ago, 'the imaginal world of meaning' (Colman, 2011).[5]

It rarely occurs to us that all these beliefs are just as much the expression of symbolic imagination as the beliefs of those once written off as 'primitive'. That is, the Cartesian world of post-Renaissance science is a particular way of *imagining* the world and the scientific method is a socially agreed practice for investigating it in terms of supposedly objective mechanisms. Even if this does occur to us, it is actually the devil's own job to think our way out of the Matrix, just as it was for Neo in the eponymous film that imagined our world as an illusion created for us by our own machines.

Participation Mystique as Lived Experience

This, it seems to me, is the real lesson from the anthropological study of indigenous cultures – not what they can learn from us but what we can learn from them. For a start, we can learn that our own ways of seeing the world are relative and that there other ways of living and thinking than those we take for granted. There is nothing like the challenge of difference to make us aware of our own presuppositions. Perhaps more deeply, though, Lévy-Bruhl's insight into *participation mystique* serves to remind us that this way of thinking and experiencing the world is not so much lost as overlooked, often reduced to a remnant that is no longer collectively represented but nevertheless still extant. In the following four examples, we can still catch a glimpse of the *anima mundi*, not as an overarching symbol but as lived experience through which, often unnoticed, we are released from our Cartesian constraints.

1   Whenever we visit the theatre or the cinema we are likely to experience states of identification in which we temporarily merge with others whom we experience as 'real people'. Similar experiences may occur listening to music, contemplating works of art or being inspired by the landscape.

2   Football matches and music festivals closely match Lévy-Bruhl's criteria for *participation mystique* as something that arises from socially organized perceptions, practices and beliefs formulated and impressed on the mind in affectively charged conditions. The 'beautiful game' expresses and reinforces ideas about competition, success and the democratic acceptance of losing that are typical of Western capitalist societies. Sporting events consist of an agreed set of social practices, rules and behaviours in which both players and spectators experience sanctioned states of high emotion that are contained and made meaningful within the context of the game.

3   Animistic beliefs persist in the tendency to impute personhood and agency to entities which according to official modernist doctrine ought to be classified as objects (Hornborg, 2006). If I had not been writing about *participation mystique* at the time, I would not have even noticed when a call-centre worker apologised for a delay, saying 'my computer is not liking me today'. Sometimes, the only explanation we can find for the way our complicated machines play up is that they must be in a bad mood[6] and we regularly experience the boundaries of our cars as coterminous with the boundaries of our own body.

4   There are some people in modern Western society – and Jung was certainly one of them – who seem to have an unusual openness and sensitivity to 'parapsychological experiences' or 'being psychic', knowing and experiencing things that are not admissible in our Cartesian world since they abrogate rules about time, space and causality. There is usually a correlation between such openness and a lack of emotional containment

in early childhood (Merchant, 2012). It seems likely that this correlation indicates areas of the psyche that remain unsocialised and unsymbolised, that slip under the radar of our collective representations. That is why they are often associated with 'borderline' states of mind, areas of experience that cannot be mentalized and express themselves in overwhelming states of unformulated affect expressed in action without thought. Like heaviness in a culture without weights, they remain unconceptualised and without apparent social usefulness. It is these states that are more successfully formulated and conceptualised within the collective representations of indigenous cultures. In such cultures people need to be able to use all the senses of their bodies to negotiate the world and so are much more attuned to aspects of the world that usually remain unsymbolised in our culture. Much of Jung's work was an attempt to provide such symbolic representations which was why he drew on pre-Cartesian traditions such as ancient myths, Gnosticism and alchemy as well as developing conceptions such as synchronicity. Unfortunately, as I have demonstrated, his work in this area was stymied by attempting to shoe-horn his theories into Kantian and Cartesian categories, not realising that these were responsible for the pinching constraints he was attempting to ease.

Conclusion

In this paper I have attempted to sketch out an alternative way forward that challenges these Cartesian constraints at their root, namely the depreciation of the body and elevation of the mind that began with Plato. I have argued that, in fact, our minds are wholly dependent on our bodies, indeed they are, as Aristotle said, merely the way our particular bodies with our very unusual brains behave in the world. Our cognition is extended and distributed and our psychic life is constituted by symbolic representations. In the final section, I have discussed the role of *participation mystique* as a way of relating to and experiencing the world that cannot be captured by the Cartesian notion of projection. It is here that we may find an opening to ways of being in the world that lead us out of the Cartesian matrix.

In conclusion, I would like to mention the work of cultural ecologist, David Abram whose book, *The Spell of the Sensuous* (1997) presents an animistic or participatory account of rationality. Abram reminds us that we are always in participation with the world in one way or another – the question is how. All too often, modern ways of being in the world keep us at one remove from the consequences of our own actions. Corporate executives in New York make decisions that decimate the lives of South American peasants; air force pilots in Texas fly drone planes that kill and maim people in the Middle East. The problem here is not commerce or warfare – the problem is the dislocation between action and embodiment, the lack of sensorial cues that feedback the consequences of action. In direct contrast to this, Abram argues for

[a] genuinely ecological approach … [that] strives to enter, ever more deeply, into the sensorial present. It strives to become ever more awake to the other lives, the other forms of sentience and sensibility that surround us in the open field of the present moment.

(Abram, 1997, p. 272)

Although, in this chapter, I have not referred to the practice of psychotherapy, I think this is also a very appropriate description for what, as psychotherapists, we strive to achieve in the daily activity of our working lives.

Notes

1 Originally published in the Journal of Analytical Psychology 62.1 (2017).
2 . . . the soul does not exist without a body and yet is not itself a kind of body. For it is not a body, but something which belongs to a body, and for this reason exists in a body, and in a body of such-and-such a kind (*De Anima* 414a20ff). https://faculty.washington.edu/smcohen/320/psyche.htm
3 Important though limited exceptions have been demonstrated in a few apes whom humans have taught to sign, notably Kanzi, the bonobo and Koko, the gorilla.
4 The phrase 'more than human world' was coined by David Abram in 1996 and, according to Wikipedia, has become 'a key phrase within the lingua franca of the ecological movement'.
5 At that time, I had not yet grasped that mind is an emergent feature of being in the world and was still talking about an interaction between mind and world, thus implying an ontological separation I would no longer accept.
6 John Cleese's portrayal of Basil Fawlty attacking his car with a branch provides an enduringly funny illustration of this only too common state of mind. (available to view on YouTube)

References

Abram, D. (1997). *The Spell of the Sensuous: Perception and Language in a More-Than-Human World.* Vintage Books.

Carpenter, A.D. (2008). Embodying intelligence. Animals and us in Plato's *Timaeus.* In *Platonism and Forms of Intelligence,* ed. John Dillon and Marie-Élise Zovko. Akademie Verlag.

Clark, A. and Chalmers, C. (1998), The extended mind. *Analysis,* 58:1, 7–19.

Colman, W. (2011). Synchronicity and the meaning-making psyche. *Journal of Analytical Psychology,* 56:4, 471–491.

Colman, W. (2015) A revolution of the mind: some implications of George Hogenson's 'The Baldwin Effect: a neglected influence on C.G. Jung's evolutionary thinking'. *Journal of Analytical Psychology,* 60:4, 520–539.

Colman, W. (2016). *Act and Image. The Emergence of Symbolic Imagination.* Spring Journal Books.

Deacon, T. (1997). *The Symbolic Species: The Co-Evolution of Language and the Brain.* W.W. Norton & Co.

Descartes, R. (2009). Letter to Princess Elisabeth, May 21, 1643. In *An Unconventional History of Western Philosophy: Conversations Between Men and Women Philosophers*, ed. K.J. Warren. Rowman and Littlefield.

Elias, N. (2011). *The Symbol Theory. Vol. 13, The Collected Works of Norbert Elias*, ed. Richard Kilminster. University College Dublin Press.

Gallagher, S. (2012). The over-extended mind. *Versus*, 113, 57–68.

Geertz, C. (1973). *The Interpretation of Cultures. Selected Essays*. Basic Books.

Hornborg, A. (2006). Animism, fetishism, and objectivism as strategies for knowing (or not knowing) the World. *Ethnos: Journal of Anthropology*, 71:1, 21–32.

Hutchins, E. (1995). *Cognition in the Wild*. MIT Press.

Jung, C.G. (1921). Psychological types. In C.G. Jung, *Collected Works, Vol. 6*. Routledge & Kegan Paul, 1971.

Jung, C.G. (1926). Spirit and life. In C.G. Jung, *Collected Works, Vol. 8*. Routledge & Kegan Paul, 2nd Edn, 1969.

Jung, C.G. (1936). Wotan. In C.G. Jung, *Collected Works, Vol. 10*. Routledge & Kegan Paul, 2nd Edn. 1969.

Jung, C.G. (1938). Psychology and religion (The Terry Lectures). In C.G. Jung, *Collected Works, Vol. 11*. Routledge & Kegan Paul, 2nd Edn. 1969.

Jung, C.G. (1939). Psychological commentary on The Tibetan Book of the Great Liberation. In C.G. Jung, *Collected Works, Vol. 11*. Routledge & Kegan Paul, 2nd Edn. 1969.

Jung, C.G. (2009). *The Red Book. Liber Novus*, ed. S. Shamdasani, trans. M. Kyburz, J. Peck, and S. Shamdasani. W.W. Norton & Co.

Lévy-Bruhl, L. (1910). *How Natives Think*, trans. Lilian A. Clare. Allen & Unwin, 1926.

Malafouris, L. (2013). *How Things Shape the Mind: A Theory of Material Engagement*. MIT Press.

Merchant, J. (2012). *Shamans and Analysts: New Insights on the Wounded Healer*. Routledge.

Plato (1951). *The Symposium*, trans. Water Hamilton. Penguin Books.

Plato (2008). *Timaeus and Critias*, trans. Robin Waterfield. Oxford University Press.

Renfrew, C. (2008). *Prehistory. The Making of the Human Mind*. Phoenix.

Searle, J. (1995). *The Construction of Social Reality*. Penguin Books.

Segal, R. (2007). Jung and Lévy-Bruhl. *Journal of Analytical Psychology*, 52:5, 635–658.

Swinburne, R. (2000). Nature and immortality of the soul. In *Concise Routledge Encyclopaedia of Philosophy*. Routledge.

Thompson, E. (2007). *Mind in Life. Biology, Phenomenology and the Sciences of Mind*. Harvard University Press.

Tomasello, M. (2008). *Origins of Human Communication*. MIT Press.

Winborn, M. (Ed.) (2014). *Shared Realities: Participation Mystique and Beyond*. Fisher King Press.

Chapter 5

J. L. Moreno's Theory of *Tele* Encounters C. G. Jung's Theory of *Synchronicity*

An Integrative Approach to Group Psychotherapy

Robin McCoy Brooks

In the early era of AIDS, I participated in the formation of a therapeutic AIDS community that radically altered my clinical and theoretical orientation as a Jungian Analyst and group psychotherapist. A nonprofit mind–body clinic named Project Quest, or Quest, was formed in 1989, for and by the community members it served.[1] During this time, I led and co-facilitated many psychodrama therapy groups and retreats while becoming credentialed as a Trainer, Educator and Practitioner (TEP) of Group Psychotherapy, Psychodrama and Sociometry.[2] I also began training to become a Jungian Analyst, so it was within the maw of AIDS that I first cut my teeth as an analyst and group leader.

It was in these contexts that I first observed how individual and group development were co-constituted through a deep engagement with each other *and* the broader psychosocial dimensions of reality to which we are inured.[3] How, I wondered, did the actual experience of living with AIDS (for example) coexist with and influence self-formation and the maturity of the group or alternatively disindividuate both? Thus, I developed a *speculative* theoretical position that considered the entirety of a situation in which we find ourselves.[4] Retaining a speculative position (as was Jung's tradition), challenged me to consider how psychical factors (universals) co-mingled with verifiable causal factors within the group as a whole, and the broader social world (as was Jacob Levy Moreno's tradition).[5] The early AIDS era was the obvious concrete *situation at hand* against which I measured the emergence of archetypal motifs (patterns, metaphor, symbols, themes, dream experiences, images, somatic expressions) that appeared in group therapy processes. I noted that archetypal motifs that emerged during an individual's psychodrama also carried a *synchronistic potential* to constellate corresponding (yet singularly apperceived) psychic states within other group members. These "meaningful coincidences,"[6] as Jung defined synchronistic events, also contributed to meaningful collective shifts in consciousness that had the potential to transform the group towards an unknown shared purpose beyond individual egoic concerns.

DOI: 10.4324/9781003429142-5

A poignant example of this phenomenon can be found in how the vision for an AIDS clinic (Quest) first manifested in the nocturnal dreams of two separate individuals, on the same night during an AIDS psychodrama retreat in the late 1980s. The dreamers, Lusijah Marx (a co-leader) and Lucas Harris (a participant) would become the co-founders of what became Project Quest because their corresponding dream visions *meaningfully resonated* with other community members, who collectively concretized the vision.[7] The Quest community, in other words, actively participated in the creation of a new consciousness from which a brick-and-mortar wellness clinic was created,

On a meta level, the "synchronistic vertex"[8] from which "Quest" emerged can be understood in the polarizing yet revolutionary context of AIDS activism, in response to dominant cultural discourses that initially denied or ignored the virus's destructive reality. While the catastrophe of AIDS was a causal factor that certainly contributed to the formation of Quest, I suggest there were synchronistic co-factors contributing to this cultural phenomenon.[9] From this perspective, I advance a notion of Jung's speculative conception of synchronicity while also taking into account the undeniable material effects of reality (AIDS, pandemics, socio-political events, ecological crisis, etc.) applied within experiential group processes. This is not a far-fetched observation. Roderick Main (2004, 2006), for example, reflects on the social significance of synchronicity for illuminating our understanding of contemporary social and cultural events. Kevin Lu and Anne Yeoman extend Main's argument for a synchronistic approach interpreting contemporary events by developing an archetypal thematic analysis (ATA) as a method they employ in qualitative research (2023).

There are few specifically Jungian and Post-Jungian scholarly contributions to *group* psychotherapy.[10] This lack—to my mind —reflects a mainstream psychoanalytic bias against the relevancy of group practice, and certainly an insufficient understanding of how group and individual unconscious processes influence each other.[11] One outstanding research exception is a volume edited by Craig Stephenson entitled *Jung and Moreno* (2014). The collection is authored by Jungian Analysts, scholars, and Jungian-oriented group therapists trained in psychodrama theory and practice who retheorize Jung's key concepts attempting to extend and deepen Jacob Levy Moreno's (1889–1974) psychodramatic technique. While certainly groundbreaking, the authors do not directly focus on Jung's theory of synchronicity or how it may interface with Moreno's concepts and group practices.[12]

My objective is to liberate Jung's individualistic model from its one-sidedness by envisioning a psychosocial self that is co-constituted from a deep engagement with "both inner and outer collective realities" (Saban, 2020, p. 97).[13] To this end, I critically engage Moreno's and Jung's distinct ontologies so as to enhance both, without conflating what is irreparably distinct.

I introduce an approach for interpreting Jung's theory of synchronicity that opens up a space to creatively explore what arises at the interface between these multiple spheres of reality (inner/outer, material/psychic, conscious/unconscious, psycho/social). While considering the causal relations between these states of mind and events, I also focus on "the possible collective meanings" that arise in a rigorous process of immanent critique within a group process (Main, 2006, pp. 49–50). I speculate that Moreno's attunement to the conscious and co-conscious dimensions of a collective, and the factors that cohere its members, presents an opportunity to identify synchronistic events that arise within a group psychotherapy process (Moreno, 1960, p. 114).

The framework for this approach provides theoretical and methodological justification for the applicability of Jung's conception of *synchronicity* in conjunction with Moreno's conception of *tele*. Tele was conceived by Moreno as a psychosocial factor that increases group cohesion and advances a mutual aid ethos. Moreno formulated his concept of tele from empirical sociometric research he conducted, that I propose intersects and deepens Jung's accounting of the relationship between the psychosocial and the constellation of archetypal patterns, within a psychotherapy group process (Moreno, 1953). Furthermore, I propose that synchronistic events hold the potential to become the psychosocial link through which the group as a whole may transform toward an unknown greater purpose.

Synchronicity as a Counterbalance to Rationalism

Jung understood that individuation was culturally contingent yet his overwhelming emphasis on the individual's intrapsychic life rather than the collective and interpersonal processes overshadowed the "psychosocial" dimension of his thought.[14] Nevertheless, his concern for society permeated his work even when he was not focusing directly on socio-political topics. Susan Rowland, for example, concludes that *The Red Book* was generated from a profound rupture in Jung's psyche, leading him to visions that revealed a plethora of splits, not only within his personal psyche, but also within the psyche of Western modernity (Rowland & Weishaus, 2021, p. 99). Sonu Shamdasani notes that in 1914, there was a shift in Jung's journal writing when he realized his visionary figures were literally, or symbolically, imbricated with culture, most auspiciously, the outbreak of the First World War on the European continent (Hillman & Shamdasani, 2013; Jung, 2012, p. 474). Peter Homans considers Jung to be a social critic, concluding that his psychology arose as a direct response to the psychosocial concerns of his era (1979/1995, pp. 175–177, in Main, 2006, p. 41).

Throughout his works, Jung was critical of war, religion, science, and other dominating cultural and academic discourses within Western modernity where rationality was privileged over imagination, intuition, creativity, nature, and spiritual presence. Jung associated the overvaluation of scientific rationalism to the problem of "mass mindedness," as most prominently elaborated in "The Undiscovered Self" (Jung, 1957/1970, para. 489; Main, 2004, 2006).[15]

Main concludes that Jung's answer to the social crises of his time was to keep the individual "from dissolving into the crowd" by creating an experientially-based psychology aimed at self-development, acquired through the many engagements with the unconscious. In this way, the individual had a fighting chance of retaining the spiritual dimension (also referred as the religious attitude) that also permeated personhood (Jung, 1957/1970, paras. 564–565).

Jung went on to view the idea of synchronicity as a counterbalance to the scientific account of the human experience (Main, 2004). According to Main, Jung's theory of synchronicity promoted experiential access to spiritual dimensions of reality in a number of ways and stated:

> In brief, these ways include supplying experiential evidence for a dimension of reality not reducible to the physical or psychic: providing a theoretical framework for understanding the autonomy and spontaneity that Jung sees as hallmarks of spirit; firming up the notion of the collective unconscious against criticisms based on the possibilities of cryptomnesia [the return of a forgotten memory, perceived as something new] or the personal origin of collective motifs; offering a means of rebutting the charge that Jung reduces God to psychology; and, above all, showing that synchronicity can be equated with numinosity and hence with the very essence of religious experience for Jung.
>
> (Main, 2006, p. 44)

Jung was not promoting a return to traditional Christianity but instead was recognizing an "alternative spirituality" where the kinds of experiences that are valid in religious experience were not reducible to organized religion (Jung, 1944/1993, paras. 1–43) and thus widely available in broader contexts.

Synchronicity Defined

Jung defined and illustrated synchronistic events in many ways, most succinctly stated as a "meaningful coincidence" (1952/1981, para. 827). Elsewhere he placed synchronistic phenomena into various categories of events, outlined below:

1   The simultaneous occurrence (or coincidence) of a certain psychic state with one or more external events which appear as meaningful parallels to the momentary subjective state (Jung, 1952/1981, para. 850) and where there is no evidence of a causal connection between the psychic state and the external event, and where considering the psychic relativity of space and time, such a connection is not even conceivable (Jung, 1957/1981, para. 984, 1952/1960, para. 526).

A personal experience comes to mind as an example. I was solo backpacking around Mt. Rainier the summer prior to analytic training—sleeping under an open sky in an ultra-light bivy sack. On the first of ten nights, I dreamed of deer, many deer, who were my companions. Upon awakening, I noted a number of deer tracks circling my head. Deer (several) had actually circled my head in the night, not my whole body but only around my head, which was peaking outside of my sleeping bag, on the bare ground. The appearance of deer figures in my dream corresponded with the simultaneous appearance of actual deer, out of my conscious awareness. The acausal connection of events (psychical and material presence of deer) and our shared sentience, had an immediate transforming effect on me that would deepen my personal analysis and training experience.

2   The coincidence of a psychic state with a corresponding (more or less simultaneous) external event taking place outside the observer's field of perception, i.e. at a distance, only verifiable afterwards (Jung, 1952/1960, para. 526).

As noted earlier, I consider the simultaneous formation of multiple activist/ empowering AIDS grassroots organizations during the first decade of AIDS as a causal co-factor and pre-condition for the synchronistic emergence of multiple activist organizations that were and were not outside of the obser-ver's field of perception. Quest was such an example. I offer a recent clinical example. A woman dreams about a colleague (who lives in another country) who was greatly distressed, so much so that the dreamer is awakened in a panic. Later that week, the dreamer texts her colleague about another matter and casually mentions her dream. The colleague is aghast as she had been, at the time of the dream, engaged in a profoundly disturbing conflict with another person with far-reaching consequences.

3   The coincidence of a psychic state with a corresponding, not yet existent future event that is distant in time and can likewise only be verified afterwards (Jung, 1957/1981, para. 850), or an unconscious image comes into consciousness either directly, i.e. literally, or indirectly (symbolized or suggested) in the form of a dream, idea, or premonition (Jung, 1957/1981, para. 858).

Jung, for example, refers to a series of waking visions about the destruction of war he had prior to the onset of the First World War (Jung, 1961/1989).

Jung's Theoretical Justification for Synchronicity

In order for Jung to clarify why synchronicity was not just a chance occur-rence, he needed to account for how certain psychological preconditions were necessary to constellate the archetype. In his later writings, Jung significantly advanced his theory of the archetype by incorporating Kantian and neo-

Kantian epistemologies to establish a demonstratable link between parallel events that contained a shared meaning (Bishop, 2000, p. 44; Brooks, 2011). Thus, Jung introduced a psyche/soma spectrum that was bridged by what he interchangeably referred to as the psychoid factor, the psychoid effect, or the psychoid archetype (Brooks, 2011). This psychic bridge was extended between material existence (phenomenal realm) on one end, and psychic existence (noumenal realm) on the other (Jung, 1946/1981, paras. 414–420). Jung located the psychoid effect of the archetype in the body, *in between* the instinctual and psychic poles (Jung, 1946/1981, paras. 376–380). He further described the psychoid factor as a "quasi" or non-psychic bridge that manifested its meaning by expressing itself in both the body *and* psychic processes. The psychoid, in other words, could not be reduced to either physical or psychic processes but had access to both. More specifically, the psychoid factor was the theoretical basis of synchronicity, and an archetype.

Thus, Jung's psychological model of the self (itself an archetype) was conceived within a broader cosmological vision that viewed psyche and matter as one unitary reality, that was the ground of all phenomena in the collective unconscious, beneath the workings of the archetypes, and whose center was the world soul or *anima mundi* (Jung, 1946/1981, paras. 388, 393, 439, in Brooks, 2011, p. 505).[16] Jung's psychoid archetype would become the *synchronistic emissary* between the world soul and the individual. The world soul was positioned as a philosophical absolute, or Archimedean point from which psyche could *observe itself* through the "organizing influences" of the constellating psychoid archetype (Jung, 1946/1981, paras. 421, 437; Jung, 1973b, p. 22; Jung, 1957/1981, para. 840). The psychoid archetype was now firmly associated with the appearance of concomitant synchronistic phenomena that enabled access to "transcendental" or "absolute" knowledge (Jung, 1957/1981, para. 948). This kind of supranatural knowledge stimulated a creative aptitude by opening the mind to new possibilities (Jung, 1957/1981, para. 912; Bishop, 2000, p. 46).

Jung also turned to analogies from quantum physics to support his psychological model of a unitary world or *Unus Mundus* by entering an intensive exchange with physicist and Nobel laureate Wolfgang Pauli (Jung & Pauli, 2014). In the 19th and 20th centuries, the wave-particle duality concept revealed that quantum entities exhibited particle and wave properties that contradicted certain features of classical physics and suspended conventional understandings of causality (Roesler & Reefshläger, 2021, pp. 7–8). Roughly summarized, light was found to behave as a wave and later to have a particle-like character; however, electrons were found to act as particles and were later discovered to have wavelike aspects. Thus, light can either manifest as a wave *or* a particle existing only in a *potential sphere* and the observance/measurement determines its concrete manifestation.

For Jung, the *Unus Mundus*, like the quantum world (or Generalized Quantum Theory), was characterized by entanglement, acausality, timelessness, and non-locality (Roesler & Reefshläger, 2021). By equating the *Unus Mundus* with the collective unconscious, Jung and Pauli hypothesized that mental states and physical states were still connected but existed only as a potential. Thus, psychical states manifested as mental or physical phenomena and under certain circumstances appeared simultaneously—identified as synchronistic. The psychoid archetypes were organized in opposites, another link to the concept of complementarity in quantum theory (Ponti & Schafer, 2013, in Roesler & Reefshläger, 2021, p. 8). From this background, Jung theorized that a synchronistic possibility was most likely to be constelled (psychoid archetype) as a correction (or compensation) for intractable unconscious one-sidedness—in an enantiodromia process. Enantiodromia occurs when the libido is blocked between seemingly unmovable forces and the conscious mind *purposefully* turns its focus to the unconscious (Jung, 1957/1970, para. 709).

Having established a unitary model of the psyche, Jung could then link the activation of an individual's synchronistic experience with the psychophysical continuum of the collective unconscious *and* the material events in world history, writing:

> The unconscious psyche responds to an individual's conscious attitude and actions, as well as to collective attitudes and events affecting that individual, through dream, fantasy images, and the occasional experience of synchronicities when the psychophysical continuum of the collective unconscious may be activated in response to collective attitudes and actions in the form of mass movements and global protest which present the symbolic "dress" of the archetype that has been constellated.
>
> (1961/1989, p. 326)

In this way, Jung considered synchronistic phenomenon as having an impact on the widest psychosocial level where events in the material world (mass movements, global protest) activate the collective unconscious and provoke the constellation of synchronicities.

Trouble in Theoretical Paradise

Jung's theoretical justification for the epistemological basis of synchronicity and psychic reality established a level of esoterism and obscurity that became "highly problematic" and at times can be accused of being incomprehensible, incoherent, incomplete, and contradictory (Bishop, 2000, p. 59; Main, 2004, pp. 36–62; Brooks, 2011). Critics of his epistemological formulations highlight his misappropriation of Kant's ontology to justify the psychoid bridge (Brooks, 2011; Huskinson, 2003; De Voogd, 1984) and his underreported reliance on the German Idealist tradition (Bishop, 2000). His reliance on Kant's foundationalist ontology to formulate a *unitary* model of psyche holds that there is a basis for knowledge derived by *a priori* postulates (absolutes).[17]

This model of understanding subjectivity disregards how contemporary psycho-social perspectives recognize the provisional, material, and social-historical contributions to human development (Brooks, 2011; Carpani, 2021). Jung's conception of a supernatural reified collective mind fails to adequately account for how particularity and universality suffuse individuality within social collectives disregarding psycho/social factors considered to be the very locus of subjective identity in the thought of Moreno and Lacan, for example (Brooks, 2023).

From these perspectives, the question arises, is the self found (*a priori* given, primordial, timeless, transcendent, absolute) or constructed (socially influenced, temporarily bound, provisional, immanent, relative) with respect to reality (Brooks, 2011; Zinkin, 1991/2008) or both? While Jung's psychoid bridge was an attempt to resolve the "mind body" question, his quest to obtain epistemological or "objective evidence" for the viability of synchronicity was wrought with "intellectual difficulties"—from the beginning for a number of reasons, including the unorthodox range of his approaches and references, the enigmatic reality of the topic, and the "inadequacy of [his] scientific training" (Jung, 1952/1981, para. 816; Main, 2004).

Post-Jungian researchers are exploring contemporary neuroevolutionary perspectives that converge with Jung's conception of a primordial-instinctual affective form of self that already exists prior to self-consciousness (Goodwyn, 2010). Alcaro et al. (2017, pp. 7, 10) reinvigorate Jung's concept of the psychoid by proposing a neuro-archetypal perspective grounded in neuro/ethological/psychological research:

> [W]e may represent core affects as "archetypes-as-such" [psychoid], primal organized configurations of intrinsically evaluative events that reveal themselves in brain-behavioral action/dispositional patterns as well as in intense affective feelings … expressing itself in the form of affective-psychic intentionality that can interact effectively, in an evaluative way, with the material, deterministic world.

In their view, affects are the primal organizers of subjective life bridging the individual's personal experiences with the collective mind and instinctual inheritance of the species. Their research indicates that subjectivity "rests on" the ancient neuropsychic processes *that humans share with animals*, noted in specific brain activity in the subcortical midline structures in various species. These processes, they suggest, are related to (prototypical) affective states that alter our awareness within a complex neuro-evolutive architecture (Alcaro et al., 2017, pp. 1, 9).[18] Their work opens the door for further considerations about the inborn and dynamic structure of the "brain-mind" and how it may lead to instinctual/behavioral actions and synchronistic psychological experiences between human beings, and humans and animals. Consider the appearance of deer in my dream, described above, and the correlating evidence the following morning that deer had actually visited me in the night.

Moreno and the Collective

I propose that Moreno's notion of tele intersects with and deepens Jung's accounting of the relationship between synchronistic events extended within a psychotherapy group. That being said, tele is not the same thing as synchronicity although these notions are easily conflated. In what follows, I orient the reader to an aerial view of Moreno's core concepts and methodologies that support Moreno's complex notion of telic relationality within the collective. These concepts are mutual aid, group cohesion, and sociometry, from which Moreno's action/ encounter methods, such as psychodrama and sociodrama, evolved.

Mutual Aid

Moreno originally conceived of group psychotherapy as a treatment for those most oppressed in society, gravitating towards working with refugees, prisoners of war, sex workers, and the severely mentally ill within their environment (Moreno, 1953). In these early group explorations, he discovered that on the psychological level, each person had the potential to be a "therapeutic agent for each other," proclaiming that each of us is a "genius" (Moreno, 2019, p. 339). Moreno was speaking from a central belief (attained from clinical experience) that everyone in a group has something to teach the group about itself *and* that everyone is a resource for each other. These early experiences opened his mind and put him on a direction toward developing a mutual aid-based group psychotherapeutic model focusing on both the individual and the socio-dynamics of the entire group (Moreno, 1953).

Moreno's development of group psychotherapy was *mutual aid*-informed in that it centered on building mutual relationships, creating an environment of social safety, and empowering person and group *in situ* (Moreno, 1953, p. 81). Until recently, the use of the term "mutual aid" was primarily limited to social activism, academics, and community and group work that has silently proliferated on the margins of psychology in the last century (Marx et al., 2025). Many of us have not been in groups whose processes are transparent, inclusive, and where everyone is encouraged to participate in group decisions. In mainstream psychology, we are not trained to care, notice, or evaluate the *group* dynamics we are participating in. It may seem difficult to imagine that we have a natural capacity to create intricate, fluid systems of mutual aid that open to multi-versal frameworks, thereby creating a culturally rich foundation for creating an environment of social safety.

A mutual aid-based climate is inclusive, participatory, collaborative, and problems are collectively engaged. Hierarchical positions are soft and not rigid. Power, or having influence and resources, is shared, not hoarded. Social cooperation and personal authenticity are not mutually exclusive but linked to social bonding that itself builds *group cohesion*. Mutual aid processes are a facilitating mechanism for group cohesion because they contribute to a sense of social safety that encourages risk-taking and authentic self-expression. Imaginary barriers to mutuality are broken down when we realize that each of us has something to contribute within a group process. Creating, modeling, teaching, and maintaining a mutual aid ethos are the heart of psychodrama group practice.

Tele, Group Cohesion, and Encounter: We are All Little Animals

Moreno's concept of tele was a means of accounting for a group's capacity to cohere and form reciprocal relationships. In his own words, "Group cohesiveness, reciprocity of relationships, communications, and shared experiences are the functions of tele" (Moreno, 1960, p. 17). A mutual aid climate fosters telic relatedness and a group's capacity to cohere. For Moreno, uncritically held transferences and projective processes initially obscure basic telic relationships, becoming a focus for exploration as people encounter each other in a group process. Repeatedly, Moreno stated that neither transference nor empathy could satisfactorily account for the ways in which group cohesion manifests (1960, p. 17, 1953, pp. 296–298). He argued that transference was based on one's inner psychodynamic experience and tele was based on the sociodynamics of two or more individuals (Moreno, 1960). In his view, transference was a "pathological portion of a universal factor" in tele, operative through the shaping and balancing of all interpersonal relationships (Moreno, 1953, p. 85).

From my perspective, balance does not mean that we iron out differences but rather that our differences can be explored in such a way that generates curiosity and unknown empathy for another group member's particular situation, point of view, or experience. Often, human commonalities (universals) emerge in the exploration of a group member's story, psychodrama, or conflict with a group member—revealing underlying telic connections. The individual, in other words, encounters their relational (self and other) attractions and repulsions within a group process. Recognizing our fundamental commonalities as human beings facilitates an awareness of our shared precarity amongst our differences.

Encounter is described by Moreno as "two persons exchanging eyes to comprehend and know each other"—a form of role reversal (1960, p. 15). The encounters between individuals and the *co-conscious and co-unconscious states* manifesting between them *is* the wellspring from which tele, transference, and empathy spring forth and can be explored (Moreno, 1961). *Group action methods* facilitate tele because they provide many opportunities for group members to encounter each other through role reversal, role playing, contact of bodies, confronting/challenging each other, sharing and loving, communicating, playing, seeing and perceiving, and participating in each other's psychodramas. Tele matures, in other words, through the multiple engagements we have with others, while also deepening our authentic relationship with ourselves. In my view, synchronicities between group members are more likely to be recognized as tele matures, and tele matures within a therapy environment that promotes social safety and regulated social/psychological engagement.

Sociometry

Moreno's observations about tele and co-factors contributing to group cohesion were derived from numerous quantitative sociometric studies of group dynamics that he rigorously developed throughout his career (Moreno, 1953, 1960). Tele is a psychosocial factor that accounts for the mutuality of choices and the absence of or increased rate of interaction between group members, and can be mapped in sociometric explorations (Moreno, 1960, p. 18). Sociometric explorations reveal the often hidden structures, agendas, subgroups, alliances, and belief systems that are operational in a group climate that hinder and/or enhance group cohesion, tele, and mutual aid practices. As described by Moreno:

> Sociometry is the mathematical study of psychological properties of population, the experimental technique of and the results obtained by application of quantitative methods ... the measurement of social phenomena ... the human individual as member of a collective is not an independent unit but a participant in collective systems and processes and the main task of mathematical methods in sociology is the quantitative analysis of such systems.
>
> (1953, pp. 15–16)

Thus, Moreno's sociometric system offers a theory of society *and* interpersonal relations in addition to providing experiential practices for assessing (telling a group about itself) and promoting change within and between individuals and the group—and ultimately society (Hale, 2009, in Giacomucci, 2021, p. 6). Group cohesion is sociometrically measured by degrees of cooperation on behalf of the unfolding purpose for which the group is formed, *without sacrificing spontaneity and creativity of the individual or sub-groupings within a group.*

Enactments; Psychodrama and Sociodrama

Psychodrama is only one leg of Jacob Levy Moreno's triadic system of sociometry, psychodrama, and group psychotherapy that offers a comprehensive approach for working with individuals, groups, and communities. Peter Felix Kellerman (1992, p. 20) composed a panoramic definition of psychodrama that I include in its entirety below, later using an actual clinical example of a psychodrama to illustrate my central points:

Psychodrama is a form of psychotherapy in which clients are encouraged to continue and complete their actions through dramatization, role-playing, and dramatic self-presentation. Both verbal and nonverbal communications are utilized. A number of scenes are enacted, depicted, for example, memories of specific happenings in the past, unfinished situations, inner dramas, fantasies, dreams, preparations for future risk-taking situations, or unrehearsed expressions of mental states in the here and now. These scenes either approximate real-life situations or are externalizations of inner mental processes. If required, other roles may be taken by group members or by inanimate objects. Many techniques are employed such as role reversal, the double, the mirror, concretizations, maximizing and soliloquy. Usually the phases of warm up, action, working through, closure and sharing can be identified.

For Moreno, the psychodrama is an elaborate form of encounter that explores the co-conscious and co-unconscious experiences of a group's members. These explorations tend to co-regulate and nurture telic connectivity (Moreno, 1960, p. 117).

Another enactment form created by Moreno is the sociodrama. The sociodrama is an action method that focuses on the whole group on a particular theme and emerges in process. A sociodrama enactment stands on its own or emerges from a psychodrama process, and vice-versa.[19] From a Jungian perspective, the psychodramatic stage provides a space for materializing psyche, in dialogue with one's depths, mind, and body—while ultimately accessing the greater wisdom of the group beyond the egoic concerns of the individual.

Jung and Moreno

Both Jung's and Moreno's distinct "holist" ontologies embraced a unified and interconnected world perspective.[20] Jung's psychological model of self was conceived within a broader cosmological perspective that viewed psyche and matter as one unitary reality whose center was a world soul or *anima mundi*. Moreno theorized a different unitary reality where the unconscious of two or more individuals was connected through an interlocking system of co-unconscious states that he extended to his group-as-a-whole approach, conceived as a fractal of the organic unity of humankind (Moreno, 1953, p. 3). Just as Moreno viewed that groups have the potential to access their common core through tele, he envisioned the existence of a common core to all of humankind that "transcended culture or language" (Giacomucci, 2021, p. 95; Moreno, 1953).[21]

Moreno tenaciously critiqued both Freud's and Jung's highly individualistic stances that were reflective of a broader tendency in the first half of the 20th century in mainstream psychology (Moreno, 1961). This stance continues to be problematic in mainstream psychology today. Moreno claimed he met Freud while attending a lecture on the interpretation of a telepathic dream at the University of Vienna in 1912. After the lecture, Moreno recalled making the following comment directly to Freud:

> Dr. Freud, I start where you leave off. You meet people in the artificial setting of your office. I meet them on the street and in their homes, in their natural surroundings. You analyzed their dreams; I try to give them courage to dream again.
>
> (Moreno et al., 1964, pp. 16–17)

Had Moreno actually met Jung, he might have said something similar to him. In lieu of an actual meeting, however, Moreno critiqued Jung's failure to consider the complementary *concrete and physical realities* that he claimed accompanied the subjective dimensions so vividly explored through psycho-dramatic methods (Moreno, 1960, p. 116, 1961, p. 2). Moreno's group psychology can be seen as a corrective for working with the destructive potential in collective human life by nurturing its creative healing potential. He *was not opposed* to Jung's idea of a collective unconscious, but critiqued Jung for not applying it to the "concrete collectivities in which we live" (Moreno, 1960, p. 116). The problem with Jung's collective unconscious, Moreno stated, "was not the collective images of a given culture or of mankind," but that Jung did not establish a "collective anchorage" for the collective unconscious. For Moreno, the collective anchorage to a shared unconscious realm can be explored through the specific relatedness (or telic health) of a group in group methods (Moreno, 1960, p. 117). To this end, he examined the possible connections between the co-unconscious states as a basis for the telic relations between two and more people.

Moreno considered the psychosocial and real-world material factors (such as AIDS, socio-political dynamics, war, poverty, etc.) to be the very site of individual and group formation. He did not isolate the individuation of the individual from its actual group relatedness. Moreno's conception of tele brings new depth to Jung's individualistic psychology because his methodologies nurture telic connectivity within group processes and consider how real-world material events also penetrate and influence how we form and transform as individuals living within the many groups in which we are embedded—across time. Moreno's ontology, in other words, establishes a real-world collective anchorage for Jung's notion of the collective unconscious.

It is important to note that Moreno *did not* incorporate Jung's conception of archetypal material into his ontology. Conceptually integrating Moreno's notion of tele with an underlying shared unconscious field such as Jung envisioned, allows us to recognize the potential for the emergence of archetypal material including synchronistic motifs (psychoid archetypes) as they may arise within a group process. Recall, Jung postulated that the emergence of synchronistic events was most likely to be constellated in an enantiodromia process (Jung, 1956/1957, para. 1586). Incorporating the significance of enantiodromia processes brings psychodynamic depth to Moreno's collective psychology as we observe its presence within group contexts. Jung described enantiodromia as a "characteristic phenomenon [that] practically dominates conscious life: in time an equally powerful counter-position is built up, which first inhibits the conscious performance and subsequently *breaks through* the conscious control" (Jung, 1957/1970, paras. 1586–1587, emphasis mine). He viewed Saul's conversion to the Apostle Paul, on the road to Damascus, as an enantiodromia experience, facilitated by the synchronistic appearance of the blinding vision and living experience of the resurrected Jesus (Brooks, 2023, pp. 56–57; Jung 1956/1957, para. 1586).

Integrating these key aspects of Jung's and Moreno's ontologies allows us to establish a psychosocial self in relation to other psychosocial selves, that are co-constituted from a deep engagement with the polarizing forces that exist between multiple spheres of reality. These multiple spheres include the inner and outer, singular and collective realities, psychical and material realities, and conscious and psychical realities, to name a few. Synchronistic motifs have the potential to enigmatically manifest within these multiple and often intersecting polarizing forces and can be mapped accordingly within a group psychotherapy process.

An Integrative Synchronistic Approach to Reading Thematic Events in Psychodrama Groups

From this background, I introduce an integrative approach for interpreting synchronistic phenomena that arise in psychodrama group processes. I retain Moreno's core belief that each group member can become a resource for each other and that the group holds the potential to heal itself. The psychodrama group is conducted within a mutual aid climate that utilizes group action methods to facilitate telic relationality and group cohesiveness and deepens personal and relational authenticity. The possibility for the emergence of synchronistic phenomena is enhanced within such a group climate. This approach is an intuitive and qualitative method that works to actively reflect various dimensions of subjective and collective realities, by exploring what is being expressed beneath the surface, *as it emerges*.

Jung's theory of synchronicity is extended as a means of interpreting the simultaneous and meaningful connections that arise between group members in a psychodramatic process, constellated by synchronistic motifs. I do not retain a strict adherence to Jung's definition of synchronistic phenomena that specifies there be "*no* evidence of a causal connection between the psychic state and … external event" (Jung, 1957/1981, para. 984, emphasis mine). Instead, I acknowledge the co-existence of causal and acasual factors that contribute to the production of synchronistic phenomena by leaning on Jung's conception of the psychoid or psychoid archetype. Jung envisioned the psychoid as a dynamic dimension of reality that exposes us to an entirety of a situation *not reducible to the physical or psychic, yet influenced by both.*[22] From my viewpoint, synchronistic phenomena emerge in-between this fluid, dynamic, neither purely psychical nor physical dimension, having the potential to meaningfully manifest within the individual and other group members.

The task of apprehending the manifestation of synchronistic phenomena and their significance to group members must be experientially verified by those affected. In other words, while the director (facilitator, therapist, analyst) may be the first to intuit or identify a synchronistic event, their interpretation of its significance must be verified by others in the group. This process becomes a reality check against the all-too-common tendency to interpret patterns of meaning that correlate with one's personal ideological, moral, or theoretical assumptions (Main, 2006, p. 51). Psychodrama group practices provide many opportunities for the director, the protagonist, and group members to verify their unique experiences of archetypal material *in situ,* and later upon reflection.

Synchronistic motifs have a universal shape and can be mapped accordingly as they arise within a group's dynamic process. Synchronistic motifs manifest as patterns, metaphors, symbols, themes, dream experiences, images, somatic expressions (shame, anxiety, speechlessness, paralysis, joy, collapse, affective arousal, heightening tensions, etc.). The manifestation of an archetypal motif is often accompanied by a turning point, a shift in consciousness, a moment of truth, a crossroads situation, a potential threshold crossing, a sudden reversal, and/or the encountering of an authentic rupture. Encountering authentic rupture, as depicted in Lacan's conception of the "Real," yields a somatic punch to the gut as we are thrown to our knees. In these situations, we are not immediately able to describe, understand, or comprehend the significance of our experience (Lacan, 2014, p. 134). For Lacan, anxiety signals an encounter with the "Real" and emerges when separation is in question, because a psychic space opens and we find ourselves in a middle between self and other (2014, p. 207). In this gap, the subject bears naked witness to fragments of a truth about its own existance because now it stands "inside and outside of [its] own picture," and is no longer entirely bound to the hegemonic discourse that was instantaneously shattered (Žižek, 2006, p. 17).

For Jung, there is a numinous, experiential quality associated with the emergence of an archetype that washes over us and cannot be put into words. The experience may be paradoxically traumatizing or open us to intense joy, wonder, or awe, akin to the Lacanian Real. The somatic qualities are deeply personal and may be accompanied by a transformative process involving a sense of connection to something larger than oneself or a radical shift in awareness. The significance of archetypes, therefore, cannot be rationally described but only "apprehended intuitively" because they are grounded in a person's embodied experience (Jung, 1951/1959, para. 301). Jung warns us that the shape that archetypes take continually changes through the ages (Jung, 1951/1959, para. 297) and therefore, their living meanings cannot be reduced to a simple or static formula (Jung, 1951/1959, paras. 301, 302).

The numinous experiential quality that Jung associated to the emergence of an archetype in individual analysis is magnified when applied to a therapy group. Within a group psychotherapy context, an encounter with the Real has the potential to open us (group member and therapist alike) to more archaic, somatic memories (possibly traumatic) or artifacts from our personal history and/or the transhistorical reservoir that may resonate with others in the group. Archetypal patterns may manifest simultaneously in the psychic states of other group members having the potential to transform the group as a whole towards an unknown greater purpose. In these situations, shared and meaningful experiences become a basis for a new consensual reality contributing to a transformational experience of the collective. The group therapist must build a therapeutic capacity to contain what is unknown, enigmatic, unrepresented, and dynamically unfolding in the collective, in the situation at hand. Such a heuristic stance creates a transitional space within the therapist that is carried into the psychodrama enactment or group process. This transitional space enables spontaneous psychic play from which we may apperceive, formulate, differentiate, and categorize information gained from *in situ* experiences— otherwise known as an immanent critique (Brooks, 2025b, 2025d).

From my perspective, archetypes are universals (shared, timeless, transcendent) that co-exist with socially relative (temporal, provisional, immanent) concrete realities. They transcend our human differences while at the same time being informed by them. While everyone in a group may be living with an AIDS diagnosis, for example, individual experiences cannot be reduced into a single explanatory category, such as an archetype of AIDS. AIDS scholar and Jungian Analyst Paul Attinello explores predominant *archetypal themes* of *death*, magnified through the many death narratives he has followed in 40 years of AIDS-related songs, memoirs, fiction, poems, and films in the urban West. Attinello (2024, p. 71) writes:

> It may seem strange that references to death from AIDS are often relatively diffuse, incomplete, and indeterminate, across 40 years ... [they] tend to shift abruptly between the terrifying and the trivial, the debased and the transcendent, and afterlives are usually ambiguous – many works project a sense that there is some kind of continuation after death, but as one we are unable to see or understand ... as though PWAs are caught between life and death, between good and evil, reflecting emotional and existential patterns familiar in psychological literature.

Attinello's analysis explores the imbedded themes and motifs in reference to death, provoked by the AIDS crisis that he claims manifested from a vacuum at the center of societal power. This psychosocial vacuum, he noted, carries with it a potential for resolution when an archetype erupts into contemporary consciousness. The liberatory emergence of Project Quest and countless other AIDS-associated grassroots organizations that arose in the first era of AIDS, and later, gives testimony to Attinello's statement. These patterns arise, Attinello notes, at the interface between polarities (enantiodromia possibilities) such as life and death, good and evil, the material and the psychical, the individual and the collective, and the inner and outer, as demonstrated in the following clinical illustration.

Group Therapy Clinical Illustration

The psychodrama process described below was conducted during a three-day residential retreat in the first era of AIDS.[23] This particular enactment demonstrates how the protagonist's exploration of an external life situation revealed an internal enantiodromia process that synchronistically affected the states and actions of other group members. I demonstrate how archetypal patterns (motifs, themes) may be identified and verified by group members as they constellate within the group as a whole, in the context of the protagonist's personal psychodrama exploration (transitional space). When the protagonist's archetypal material appeared to be affecting the states and actions of other group members, I expanded the frame of the psychodrama into a sociodrama. I refer to the protagonist as Brian, to disguise his identity.[24]

Brian arose and slowly walked to the workspace in the room (the psychodramatic stage) where I joined him. We briefly looked into each other's eyes and a feeling of infinite sadness pulled me into a swirling eddy. I shuddered involuntarily, needing to ground my feet on the floor to remain steady. He too, I noticed, was wobbling on his feet. *"I'm right here,"* I said. *"I am with you, Brian ... May I put my hand on your back?"* He nodded, yes. And then I asked him, *"How may we help you today?"* With mounting urgency, Brian blurted out his dilemma. *"I want a lover, for the first time in my life ... before I die."* Adding: *"I know this is impossible because I am dying."* On the surface of things, Brian's bold and desperate plea for a lover was seemingly impossible, hopeless. His dilemma, as it turned out, reflected a lifelong void plagued with impossible desires.

I asked Brian if he felt stable enough on his feet to walk the periphery of the workspace together. He nodded, yes. During our slow promenade I asked him to tell me about a time in his life that he remembered feeling safe. Brian balked at the question and stopped walking, giving me a bewildering look, as if to say, *"What has safety got to do with this,"* or, *"What is safety?"* From his look, I said: *"My question grew from your comment that you had not ever experienced a loving relationship."*

With that, he started walking again and I stayed with him. Slowly, Brian agonizingly squeezed out few details about his relational life. *"I don't want to talk about them, my family,"* he stridently stated. *"Okay,"* I answered. When he spoke, his eyes welled up with tears and he reflexively wiped his snotty nose on his sleeve. A group member hopped up giving him a tissue, and Brian accepted it with a nod. He shared that he had always been single, lived alone, and before he was sick, had a few fuck buddies—*"but that is over now because I can't get it up,"* he added, with a sardonic laugh. Others in the room, I noted, nervously laughed with him. *"Did you hear others laughing with you just now?"* I asked. *"Maybe you are not alone."* I then asked group members to raise their hands if they were afraid of, or had already experienced, sexual difficulties since their diagnosis. Many hands slowly raised. Brian slowly looked around the room, nodding. I thanked the group for their honesty.

At this point, I asked Brian to imagine what a lover could be like, now. Again, he stopped walking and looked at me blankly. *"Are you having difficulty imagining how you can be loved now?"* I added. His shoulders collapsed, and his face fell even further into that bottomless maw of grief.

This psychodrama could be seen as a last-stop plea to fill Brian's gaping loveless void before his death. We did not have the kind of time to untangle what I hypothesized were symptoms of developmental trauma, further complicated by societal trauma due to Brian's gay orientation and now AIDS diagnosis—a lifelong social isolate, a societal leper-thing who, as it turned out, had not completely given up. In between the oppositional tensions of lack and impending death, Brian's tenacious desire manifested in the signifier "lover." He did not have language to define what he had not viscerally experienced ... yet his desire for love in the face of its impossibility, not only survived, but courageously hoisted itself into the group space.

Love is what he wants, I thought. Mutual love. Who amongst us doesn't need love? A space in my mind opened to a new direction *where love's impossibility crashes into a psychophysical possibility.* Following my intuition, I said: *"I have an idea of how we can explore your desire for love in action, Brian. Are you open?"* Looking at me with what appeared to be faint relief, he nodded, yes.

I turned toward the group. *"Who is available to play the role of Brian's lover?"* I asked. Hands raised, one at a time. Soon, everybody was raising their hands. *Everybody.* Imagine a field full of dandelions, suddenly bursting into bloom. Electricity ignited the group. How can we understand the loving animation that mobilized such a collective response, except through tele. At this point, I began to suspect that Brian's desire for love was constellating amongst the group as a whole. While retaining my focus on Brian's unfolding psychodrama, I began to shift my attention to how I could also include the whole group thus expanding the frame to a psychodrama *within* a sociodrama.

I coached Brian to look into each of his group members' faces, who still had raised hands. *"Take in what you see here,"* I said. Tears welled in his eyes, and I thought he might faint. Hand on his back, I then directed Brian to select a person from the group to play the role of his lover, and he did. *"Describe the scene,"* I said. *"I want to eat popcorn in bed with my lover, watching TV,"* he immediately replied. There was a rumble of genuine laughter in the room, and a slight smile appeared on Brian's gaunt face. After he set up the scene, I asked him to *play the role* of his psychodramatic lover. *"Show us how you want to be loved, Brian,"* I said, as he played the role of his own lover. After a few adjustments, I reversed Brian back to being himself. The Lover auxiliary played out the scene with Brian, as he had set it up.

After a few minutes, I asked the group: *"Stand up if you would like to role reverse into this scene?"* Everyone stood up. *"Take a look at this ...,"* I told Brian, *"you are tapping into a collective reservoir!"* I then asked Brian to step out of the scene, as the first volunteer immediately stepped into it, instructing the new couple to keep the scene going as I set up another couple scene, with Brian. In this manner, I eventually paired each group member with Brian—who each time, created new ways of giving and receiving love with his role players. At the same time, I encouraged the role players to extend what Brian had personally created, into a scene that each person wanted to experience.

John Olesen, my colleague and a participant of the group, remembers "the collective spell" that fell over the entire group during this process (Olesen, 2025). Brian manifested and received many kinds of loving experiences with everybody in the group. Everyone in the group experienced reciprocal nurturing. We were all "lovers" now.

While disease could not be cured, the protagonist's suffering from love's negation could be remedied. Love was the remedy. We cannot legislate love. Brian's lifelong yearning for love amidst its impossibility simultaneously activated a collective desire for loving care from each member of the group. The individual stories from which this desire arose would later be recalled and some enacted throughout the retreat.

The participants were all worn down from a collective loss of *Eros.* In this room, however, love became a medicine for collective exile, marginalization, disempowerment, and imminent death. Subversive love; love as activism; returning to the memory of wholeness through love; love as a socio-political-systemic correction; love as an archetype; numinous love. The psychodrama transformed into a reparative sociodramatic ceremony for the group, where forbidden, impossible, and lost love is found again, or newly experienced. Life's sacredness is momentarily restored.

Upon Closing

In summary, the psychic states of one person, a collective, and a society have the potential to synchronistically co-affect the psychic states or actions of others within a psychotherapy group and/or community. Often, the traumatic experience of living with an AIDS diagnosis opened group participants to experiences of underlying childhood traumatic histories that impaired their capacities to acquire a sense of social safety or engage in mutual relationships.

Mutual aid-based groups, as described above, become containers through which we explored the activated responses (dreams, desires, fantasy images, somatic expressions, etc.) that arose from a shared psychophysical reality. Polarizing external social-political realities generated from the widest psychosocial contexts may constellate an internal enantiodromia experience within the individual and likewise constellate shared synchronistic experiences amongst group members. When recognized, synchronicities carry the potential to restore a sense of social significance because, in the words of Main, they "dignify the evidence of interconnectedness that transcends ordinary social and cultural interactions" (Main, 2006, p. 49). We are reminded of our shared humanity, in other words. When awakened, our shared precarity carries with it the potential to collectively transcend degrading social interactions that deny or ignore human suffering and the sacredness of life.

Notes

1 Project Quest exists today and is now named the Quest Center for Integrative Health, in Portland, Oregon. Quest provides integrative healthcare services, community, and education with a wellness-focused approach to living.

2 For the sake of efficiency, from this point onward, I refer to Jacob Levy Moreno's triadic theoretical and clinical system of group psychotherapy, psychodrama, and sociometry as "psychodrama."

3 Elsewhere, I describe Gilbert Simondon's radical notion of psychosocial individuation referred to as transindividuality. Simondon viewed psychic individuation as a social process whereby the subject reached beyond itself, leading itself toward others in a wider system of word, then folded back into itself in order to amplify the processes of differentiation repeatedly through life (Brooks, 2023 pp. 16-25). For Simondon, the phenomenon of collective individuation was the true psychosocial from which the trans individual arises (Simondon, 1992, pp. 248, 302).

4 I lean here on Greg Mogenson's elaboration of a speculative form of theorizing the psyche. "According to this tradition [Speculative philosophy], concepts [archetypal] such as "soul," "truth", "love," "friendship," "Freedom," and "justice," etc, are to be continually measured against themselves in the situation at hand, which is also to say, defined and redefined via a rigorous process of immanent critique" (Mogenson, 2023, p. 6 fn. 16). By "speculative" I refer to the tradition of Speculative philosophy (Kant, Fichte, Schelling, Hegel, Schopenhauer to name a few) . It is well beyond the scope of this essay to engage in a comprehensive discussion regarding divergent and intersecting traditions within so called speculative philosophy or how Jung was influenced by these philosophy traditions (see Mills, 2019, Clarke, 1992, Bishop, 1999). Most generally speaking, speculative philosophy seeks to obtain a comprehensive understanding and explanation of the structural interrelations to the whole of reality, the nature of the universe and what it means to be human. Further, it is a form of theorizing that does not rely on empirical evidence or verifiable observation evidence (Audi, 1995 p. 759). The tendency to marginalize concrete particularities of the natural and social world remains a central concern for contemporary critics, including myself (Brooks, 2011, 2019, 2023, 2025). This critique has begun to attract the attention contemporary Jungian scholars interested in extending in developing a psychosocial self within the many intersecting dimensions of reality, including the contributors of this book. See footnote 11.

5 By "speculative" I refer to the tradition of speculative philosophy (Kant, Fichte, Schelling, Hegel, Schopenhauer to name a few) . It is well beyond the scope of this essay to engage in a comprehensive discussion regarding divergent and intersecting traditions within so called speculative philosophy or how Jung was influenced by these philosophy traditions (see Mills, 2019, Clarke, 1992, Bishop, 1999). Most generally speaking, speculative philosophy seeks to obtain a comprehensive understanding and explanation of the structural interrelations to the whole of reality, the nature of the universe and what it means to be human. Further, it is a form of theorizing that does not rely solely on empirical evidence or verifiable observation evidence (Audi, 1995 p. 759). The tendency to marginalize concrete particularities of the natural and social world remain a central concern of its contemporary critics, including myself (Brooks, 2011, 2019, 2023, 2025a, b). This critique has begun to attract the attention contemporary Jungian scholars, including the contributors of this book. See footnote 13.

6 Jung, 1952/1981, para. 829.

7 Lusijah Marx describes this event at length and the environment from which it arose (Marx, 2025). Lucas Harris died of AIDS seven years after Quest became a non-profit center in 1989.

8 I borrow this term from Lu and Yeoman, 2023, p. 31.

9 Quest was only one of many grass-roots activist projects to simultaneously emerge across the United States (and elsewhere), in response to the large scale governmental/societal denial about the psychological and medical realities incurred from the rapidly spreading virus. Other AIDS related grass roots volunteer organizations were simultaneously forming in response to the vacuum of aid (Denver Principles, 1983; France, D. 2016; Schulman, S., 2021). Grass roots activist groups, many of which were mutual aid oriented (Schulman, 2021) targeted US Food and Drug Administration, the pharmaceutical industry, and unresponsive and hostile governments by publicly *visibilizing* and advocating for the needs and realities of PWA. Many of these liberatory efforts were organized by PWA's and their allies. It is not within the scope of this essay to develop an argument to support the viability of this psychosocial phenomenon in this essay.

10 Further, Siyat Ulon - psychiatrist and Jungian oriented therapist, scholar and Trainer Educator and Practitioner of Group Psychotherapy, Sociometry and Psychodrama (TEP) practices medicine and trains students of psychodrama in Taiwan. See Ulon & Brooks (2018). Additionally, Italian Jungian Analyst and psychologist Maurizio Gasseau regularly teaches and directs psychodramas internationally.

11 Psychoanalysis' century old focus on individual treatment contradicts our psychological reliance on group processes in human development throughout our lifetime. We train in groups in analytic institutes, we teach and learn in groups in the academy, and we congregate professionally in groups. Implicit biases are prevalent within the broader field of psychology, as well, as it was only in 2018, when the American Psychological Association, formally recognized group psychology and group psychotherapy as a specialty area, creating new possibilities for its inclusion in educational and certifying programs (Whittingham, Lefforge, Marmaroch, 2021).

12 While synchronicity is referenced indirectly (Stephenson, 2014, pp. 171, 176) there is no in-depth theoretical exploration of the concept or correlation to Moreno's conception of tele, although tele is discussed separately, at some length.

13 Additional Post-Jungian approaches connected to contemporary psychosocial discourses are Brewster, 2019; Hopcke, R., 2009; Samuels, 2015; Papadopoulos, 2002; Singer & Kimbles, 2004), Watkins, 2019, to name only a few.

14 Jungian Analyst and Child Psychoanalyst Michael Fordham commented on Jung's obsession with the psyche. Fordham recalls attempting to discuss child therapy at a dinner party with the Jungs. Of Jung, Fordham stated: "He was starting on a monologue when Mrs. Jung intervened: "You know very well that you are not interested in people, but [only] your theory of the collective unconscious" (Fordham, 1975, 102-113). Psychosocial studies, as I am using the term here is an intellectual transdisciplinary tradition that reaches across psychology, sociology and related disciplines that include, postcolonial studies, queer studies, feminism, anthropology, philosophy (Frosh, 2019, Frosh & Baraitser, 2008, p. 348).The origins of this mode of psychosocial studies were derived from Western European traditions of critical social psychology and sociology, critical theory, political and social psychoanalysis (Frosh, 2019). I consider luminaries of group and community psychology from the last century to be pioneers of the psychesocial. These include J. L. Moreno, Ignacio Martín-Baró, founder of Liberation Psychology in the Global South, and William Schwartz, who amongst other social workers in the U. S. introduced the concept and practices of mutual aid in their approaches to community and group psychology (Brooks, R. M. 2025a).

15 Main (2006, p. 41) summarizes three interlocking features one of the prevailing theories of mass society (in addition to Marx) in Jung's era, originated in Max Scheler, José Ortega, and Karl Mannheim, outlined by Homans (1979/1995). Both (Main and Homans) concluded that Jung's understanding of mass society was very similar to that of the theory of mass society especially articulated in "The Undiscovered Self" (1957/1970).

16 For example, Jung stated in Letters 1, p. 256 – "The psyche does not exist wholly in time and space. It is very probable that only what we call consciousness is contained in space and time, and the rest is psyche. The unconscious exists in a state of relative spacelessness and timelessness. For the psyche, this means a relative eternality and relative non-separation from other psyches, or a oneness with them." Jung illustratively correlated the concept of a psyche/soma spectrum that was bridged by the psychoid with the symbolic image of the tail-eating Uroborus (1946/1981, para 416)

17 Ladson Hinton warns us of the dangers inherent in a unitary cosmology when he states: "When the ideal is unity [Unus Mundus] there is always the tendency to abject those who are cast as preventing the achievement of Utopia. The horror of genocide is a prism that magnifies the all-too-human tendency to eliminate the troubling "other," whom we blame for disrupting our personal or social worlds" (Hinton, 2011, p. 380).

18 I cannot adequately represent the rigorous research upon which Alcaro, Carta and Panksepp make their claims and encourage the reader to follow their work.

19 A sociodrama investigates the intergroup relations and collective ideologies that shape these relations and exposes us to our critically held unconscious narratives that we hold that shape our relations enabled by childhood experiences and psycho-social, cultural norms. See Ulon & Brooks, R. M., 2018, for a theoretical accounting of sociodrama and case illustration of a sociodrama we conducted during an International Association for Jungian Studies Conference, in Cape Town, South Africa, in 2017.

20 See Holism Possibilities and Problems, edited by Christian MacMillan, Roderick Main and David Henderson (2020) for a comprehensive, multi-disciplinary and critical reflection on the historicity, meanings, applications and implications of Holistic thought, including Jung's ontology.

21 Moreno's the cosmic person as "an individual who is close to all being, not really apart from them but with them and within them, involved with all [persons],

animals and plants. Consider the neuro/ethical/psychological research of Alcaro (et al.) discussed above who argue for a shared synchronistic psychological experience between human beings and humans and animals. Returning to Moreno,, he believed himself to belong to a universe not as a member of a family or clan because everyone was a brother or partner. In his work, he did make the distinction between socio-economic class, gender, race etc, because he wanted to help everyone and make his methods available to everyone, as his lifework indicates (Moreno, J. L., 2009, p. 339, Brooks, R. M. 2025 a).

22 This is not the place to reiterate my critique of Jung's epistemological justification for his later formulation of the psychoid archetype (See Brooks, 2011). However, there are aspects of his justification for the existence of synchronistic phenomena that I accept and extend into the psychosocial realm.

23 I rework my recollection of a psychodrama I directed during an AIDS retreat over 30 years ago from Chapter 9 in *The Healing Power of Community: Mutual Aid, AIDS & Social Transformation* (2025 b) Routledge. Johnny Oleson, the author of the book's Foreword, first referred to this specific psychodrama. In the present chapter, I refer to same psychodrama but reconceptualize my description to illustrate a synchronistic approach to thematic analysis as it is enhanced by Moreno's concept of tele. There remains a fictional quality to memory-recall and this is especially true in remembering dialogue that occurred over 30 years ago. What dialogue I could not actually remember, I substitute with the feeling of what was happening, in conjunction with the recall of Johnny Oleson, who was also there.

24 I remain grateful to the young man I refer to as Brian in this case illustration. I am grateful for his life and the courage he demonstrated to fight for what he needed in the face of its impossibility. Brian died shortly after this retreat.

References

Alcaro, A., Carta, C., & Panksepp, J. (2017). The Affective Core of the Self: A Neuro-Archetypal Perspective on the Foundations of Human (and Animal) Subjectivity. *Frontiers in Psychology*, 8(1424). doi:10.3389/fpsyg.2017.01424

Atmanspacher, H., Römer, H., & Walach, H. (2002). Weak Quantum Theory: Complementarity and Entanglement in Physics and Beyond. *Foundations of Physics*, 32, pp. 379–406.

Attinello, P. (2024). Splintered Afterlives: AIDS, Death and Beyond. In E. Brodersen (Ed.), *Jungian Dimensions of the Mourning Process, Burial Rituals and Access to the Land of the Dead Intimations of Immortality*. Routledge.

Audi, R. (Ed.) (1995). *The Cambridge Dictionary of Philosophy*. Cambridge University Press.

Bishop, P. (2000). *Synchronicity and Intellectual Intuition in Kant, Swedenborg, and Jung*. The Edwin Mellen Press.

Brewster, F. (2019). *The Racial Complex: A Jungian Perspective on Culture and Race*. Routledge.

Brooks, R.M. (2011). Un-thought Out Metaphysics in Analytical Psychology: A Critique of Jung's Epistemological Basis for Psychic Reality. *Journal of Analytical Psychology*, 56, pp. 492–513.

Brooks, R.M. (2019). A Critique of C. G. Jung's Theoretical Basis for Selfhood Theory Vexed by Incorporeal Ontology. In J. Mills (Ed.), *Jung and Psychology*. Routledge.

Brooks, R.M. (2023). *Catastrophe, Psychoanalysis and Social Change*. Routledge.

Brooks, R.M. (2025a). Luminaries of Group and Community Psychology. In L. Marx, G. Harriman, & R.M. Brooks, *The Healing Power of Community: Mutual Aid, AIDS & Social Transformation in Psychology*. Routledge.

Brooks, R.M. (2025b). Contemporary Applications of Jung's Method of Active Imagination in Activist Arts-Based Research and Psychodrama. In L. Marx, G. Harriman, & R.M. Brooks, *The Healing Power of Community: Mutual Aid, AIDS & Social Transformation in Psychology*. Routledge.

Brooks, R.M. (2025c). A Brief History of U.S. Mutual Aid Movements. In L. Marx, G. Harriman, & R.M. Brooks, *The Healing Power of Community: Mutual Aid, AIDS & Social Transformation in Psychology*. Routledge.

Brooks, R.M. (2025d). Group Therapy, Psychodrama and Community Building. In L. Marx, G. Harriman, & R.M. Brooks, *The Healing Power of Community: Mutual Aid, AIDS & Social Transformation in Psychology*. Routledge.

Carpani, S. (2021). Introduction – Andrew Samuels: Plurality, Politics and the "Individual". In S. Carpani (Ed.), *The Plural Turn in Jungian and Post-Jungian Studies: The Work of Andrew Samuels*, pp. 1–12. Routledge.

Clarke, J.J. (1992). *In Search of Jung*. Routledge.

Denver Principles. (1983). *Act Up Historical Archive*: https://actupny.org/documents/Denver.html

De Voogd, S. (1984). Fantasy versus Fiction: Jung's Kantianism Appraised. In R. Papadopoulos & G. Saayman (Eds.), *Jung in Modern Perspective*, pp. 204–228. Wildwood House.

Fordham, M. (1975). Memories and Thoughts About C. G. Jung. *Journal of Analytical Psychology*, 20, pp. 102–113.

France, D. (2016). *How to Survive a Plague – The Story of How Activists and Scientists Tamed AIDS*. Alfred A. Knopf.

Frosh, S. (2019). Psychosocial Studies with Psychoanalysis. *Journal of Psychosocial Studies*, 12(1–2), pp. 101–114.

Frosh, S. & Baraitser, L. (2008). Psychoanalysis and Psychosocial Studies. *Psychoanalysis, Culture & Society*, 13, pp. 346–365.

Giacomucci, S. (2021). *Social Work, Sociometry, and Psychodrama Experiential Approaches for Group Therapists, Community Leaders, and Social Workers*. Springer.

Goodwyn, E. (2010). Approaching Archetypes: Reconsidering Innateness. *Journal of Analytical Psychology*, 55, pp. 502–521.

Hale, A. (2009). Moreno's Sociometry: Exploring Interpersonal Connection. *Group*, 33 (4), pp. 347–358.

Hillman, J. & Shamdasani, S. (2013). *Lament of the Dead: Psychology after Jung's Red Book*. W.W. Norton.

Hinton, L. (2011). Unus Mundus – Transcendent Truth or Comforting Fiction? Overwhelm and the Search for Meaning in a Fragmented World. *Journal of Analytical Psychology*, 56(3), pp. 375–380.

Homans, P. (1979/1995). *Jung in Context: Modernity and the Making of a Psychology*. The University of Chicago Press.

Hopcke, R. (2009). Synchronicity and Psychotherapy: Jung's Concept and Its Use in Clinical Work. *Psychiatric Annals*, 39(5), pp. 287–296.

Huskinson, L. (2003). *Nietzsche and Jung: The Whole Self in the Union of Opposites*. Brunner-Routledge.

Jung, C.G. (1944/1993). Introduction to the Religious and Psychological Problems of Alchemy. In *Collected Works, Vol. 12. Psychology and Alchemy* (pp. 1–37). Princeton University Press.

Jung, C.G. (1946/1981). On the Nature of the Psyche. In *Collected Works, Vol. 8. The Structure and Dynamics of the Psyche* (pp. 520–531). Princeton University Press.

Jung, C.G. (1951/1959). The Psychology of the Child Archetype. In *Collected Works, Vol. 9i. The Archetypes of the Collective Unconscious* (pp. 151–181). Princeton University Press.

Jung, C.G. (1952/1960). On Synchronicity. In *Collected Works, Vol. 8. The Structure and Dynamics of the Psyche* (pp. 520–531). Routledge & Kegan Paul.

Jung, C.G. (1952/1981). Synchronicity: An Acausal Connecting Principle. In *Collected Works, Vol. 8. The Structure and Dynamics of the Psyche* (pp. 419–519). Routledge & Kegan Paul.

Jung, C.G. (1956/1957). Jung and Religious Belief. In *Collected Works, Vol. 18. The Symbolic Life* (pp. 707–744). Routledge & Kegan Paul.

Jung, C.G. (1957/1970). The Undiscovered Self. In *Collected Works, Vol. 10. Civilization in Transition*. Routledge & Kegan Paul.

Jung. C.G. (1957/1981). On Synchronicity. In *Collected Works, Vol. 8: The Structure and Dynamics of the Psyche* (pp. 520–531). Princeton University Press.

Jung, C.G. (1957/1983). Alchemical Studies. In *Collected Works, Vol. 13. Commentary on "The Secret of the Golden Flower"* (pp. 6–56). Princeton University Press.

Jung, C.G. (1961/1989). *Memories, Dreams, Reflections* (R. Jaffe & C. Winston, Trans.). Pantheon Books.

Jung, C.G. (1973a). *Letters of C. G. Jung Vol. I*. Routledge and Kegan Paul.

Jung, C.G. (1973b). *Letters of C. G. Jung Vol. II*. Routledge and Kegan Paul.

Jung, C.G. & Pauli, W. (2014). *Atom and Archetype: The Pauli/Jung Letters, 1932–1958*. Princeton University Press.

Kellerman, P.F. (2007). *Sociodrama and Collective Trauma*. Jessica Kingsley Publishers.

Lacan, J. (2014). *Anxiety: The Seminar of Jacques Lacan, Book X* (J. A. Miller & A. R. Price, Trans.). Polity Press.

Lu, K. & Yeoman, A. (2023). The Future of Jungian Psycho-Social Studies: Akira, Greta Thunberg and Archetypal Thematic Analysis (ATA). *International Journal of Jungian Studies*, 16.

Main, R. (2004). *The Rupture of Time*. Brunner-Routledge.

Main, R. (2006). The Social Significance of Synchronicity. *Psychoanalysis, Culture & Society*, 11, pp. 36–53.

Marx, L. (2025). Project Quest's Story. In L. Marx, G. Harriman, & R.M. Brooks, *The Healing Power of Community: Mutual Aid, AIDS & Social Transformation in Psychology*. Routledge.

Marx, L., Harriman, G., & Brooks, R.M. (2025). *The Healing Power of Community: Mutual Aid, AIDS & Social Transformation in Psychology*. Routledge.

McMillan, C., Main, R., & Henderson, D. (Eds.) (2020). *Holism Possibilities and Problems*. Routledge.

Mills, J. (Ed.) (2019). *Jung and Philosophy*. Routledge.

Mogenson, G. (2023). *Vicarius Anime Speculative I - Statement in Jungian Psychotherapy*. Dusk Owl Books.

Moreno, J.L. (1953). *Who Shall Survive: Foundations of Sociometry, Group Psychology and Sociodrama*. Beacon House Inc.

Moreno, J.L. (1960). Sociometric Base of Group Psychotherapy. In J.L. Moreno et al. (Eds.), *The Sociometry Reader*. The Free Press.

Moreno, J.L. (1961). Interpersonal Therapy and Co-Unconscious States, A Progress Report in Psychodrama Theory. *Group Psychotherapy*, 14(3–4), pp. 234–241.

Moreno, J.L. (2019). *The Autobiography of a Genius* (E. Schreiber, S. Kelley, & S. Giacomucci, Eds.). North West Psychodrama Association.

Moreno, J.L., Moreno, Z.T., & Moreno, J.D. (1964). The First Psychodramatic Family. *Group Psychotherapy*, 16, pp. 203–249.

Oleson, J. (2025). Foreword. In L. Marx, G. Harriman, & R.M. Brooks, *The Healing Power of Community: Mutual Aid, AIDS & Social Transformation in Psychology*. Routledge.

Papadopoulos, R. (2002). *Therapeutic Care for Refugees: No Place Like Home*. Karnac.

Ponti, D.V. & Schafer, L. (2013). Carl Gustav Jung, Quantum Physics and the Spiritual Mind: A Mystical Vision of the 21st Century. *Behavioral Sciences*, 3, pp. 601–618.

Roesler, C. & Reefshläger, G., (2021). Jungian Psychotherapy, Spirituality, and Synchronicity: Theory, Applications, and Evidence Base. *Psychotherapy Theory Research Practice Training*, 3, pp. 339–350.

Rowland, S. & Weishaus, J. (2021). *Jungian Arts-Based Research and the Nuclear Enchantment of New Mexico*. Routledge.

Saban, M. (2020). Simondon and Jung: Rethinking Individuation. In C. McMillan, R. Main, and D. Henderson (Eds.), *Holism Possibilities and Problems*, pp. 91–97. Routledge.

Samuels, A. (2015). Global Politics, American Hegemony and Vulnerability and Jungian Psychosocial Studies: Why There Are No Winners in the Battle Between Trickster Pedro Urdemales and the Gringos. *International Journal of Jungian Studies*, 7(3), pp. 227–241.

Schulman, S. (2021). *Let the Record Show – A Political History of Act Up New York 1987–1993*. Farrar, Straus and Giroux.

Simondon, G. (1992). The Genesis of the Individual. In J. Crary & K. Winter Sanford (Eds.), *Incorporations*, pp. 297–319. Zone.

Singer, T. & Kimbles, S. (Eds.) (2004). *The Cultural Complex: Contemporary Jungian Perspectives on Psyche and Society*. Brunner-Routledge.

Stephenson, C.E. (2014). *Jung and Moreno: Essays on the Theatre of Human Nature*. Routledge.

Ulon, S. & Brooks, R.M. (2018). Collective Shadows on the Sociodrama Stage. *International Journal of Jungian Studies*, 10.

Watkins, M. (2019). *Mutual Accompaniment and the Creation of the Commons*. Yale University Press.

Whittingham, M., Lefforge, N., & Marmarosh, C. (2021). Group Psychotherapy as a Specialty: An Inconvenient Truth. *Group Psychology and Group Psychotherapy*, 74(2), pp. 60–66.

Zinkin, L. (1991/2008). Your Self: Did you Find it or Did you Make it? *Journal of Analytical Psychology*, 53(3), pp. 389–408.

Žižek, S. (2006). *The Parallax View*. MIT Press.

Chapter 6

The Dynamics and Ethic of the Deep Relational Self

Marcus West

This chapter discusses how it is that the Jungian project of the development of (the) self is essentially deeply relational and yet how, for a time at least, the individual will likely turn inward, perhaps needing to stand against relationships which do not very closely mirror and support the expression of self (those which are experienced as 'other'—see for example Kohut's (1971) discussion of the need for a 'selfobject'). This applies on the individual level, for example, in relation to the analyst, as well as societal level, standing against collective norms, as Jung described in relation to the process of individuation (Jung, 1939). This process allows us to live more true to ourselves and fulfil our call to wholeness, reclaiming parts of the self lost through the process of socialisation, which begins from the first breaths of life.

The chapter then describes how this involutionary/inward-turning process leads to a deeper connectedness, which became lost in the process of socialisation (where compliance became a substitute for true connectedness). It leads to a recognition of our symmetry with others, which carries a deeper resonance with them and has its own relational ethic.

From this comes a more profound socialisation that is both soulful, self-centred and selfless at the same time. It is living primarily from the Self, in the sense that Jung (1951) used the term to refer to the overarching totality of the self (much of which operates unconsciously), rather than the ego. It is living in synchronistic connection with others, in tune with the spirit of the depths that enriches, enlivens, and develops the zeitgeist, the spirit of the times (Jung, 2009, p. 229).

Introduction

Jung describes the need, at times, to stand against the collective in the process of individuation (1939). I will focus here on how this can occur at a moment-by-moment, personal level, including in the analytic relationship, in the service of the individual coming more fully into being. As Jung wrote: 'This resistance [to the analyst] arises from the demand for individuation, which is *against* all adaptation to others' (Jung, 1916/1964, paras. 1094–1095, emphasis in the original).

DOI: 10.4324/9781003429142-6

The Jungian analytic attitude, as sometimes (but not always) practiced, aims to address this conflict precisely by accompanying the individual in such a way as to allow the patient to inclusively accept, encompass and reclaim the parts of the self that have lain dissociated and/or abhorred in the shadow. As Jung put it in his excellent paper, 'The therapeutic value of abreaction':

> Not only must the patient be able to see the cause and origin of his neurosis, he must also see the legitimate psychological goal towards which he is striving. We cannot simply extract his morbidity like a foreign body, lest something essential be removed along with it, something meant for life. Our task is not to weed it out, but to cultivate and transform this growing thing until it can play its part in the totality of the psyche.
>
> (Jung, 1921/1928, para. 293)

This analytic attitude, based on acceptance, allows the patient to discover that, 'his own unique personality has value, that he has been accepted for what he is, *and that he has it in him to adapt himself to the demands of life*' (Jung, 1921/1928, para. 290, emphasis mine). I have italicised the last phrase of the quote to highlight the fact that the analyst's acceptance of the patient's distinct personality, facilitating the patient's acceptance of themselves, allows a reorientation towards the social world.

The Involutionary Phase

I will deal first with the inward-turning aspect of the journey—to discover, accept and integrate the lost parts of ourselves.

Whilst we can know about parts of ourselves privately and/or intellectually, in order for these parts to come fully into being, to be lived from in an enlivening way and integrated into our personality, they need to be brought into relationship with another person. This perhaps reflects our primitive, relational biology—that our psyches are primed to engage with and, to a significant extent, *fit in with* our caregivers as a matter of survival and as part of the process of adaptation to the relational/social environment.

Our upbringing necessarily takes place in relation to others, whether that is in a nuclear, extended or foster family, or a childcare institution, all of which exist within, and are influenced by, the wider culture and society. Through repetition, as the child develops, they learn which elements of themselves are responded to, welcomed and accepted, and which are met with an adverse response. This includes getting no response at all, or even persistent intrusion by the caregiver's otherness (driven by the caregiver's own needs), displacing the child's own natural idiom (these processes are described in fine detail in Tronick, 2007; BCPSG, 2010).

If adverse reactions to particular forms of self-expression are met with frequently enough, those parts of the self are split off and dissociated from the ego through the operation of a primitive superego, which closes down and inhibits self-expression. Later on, in more sophisticated forms, this inhibition occurs through the operation of shame.

What is acceptable to the caregiver will also have been influenced in some way by their particular culture. And even if the caregiver stands against a particular cultural norm, for example, attitudes toward gender or sexual orientation, the individual themselves will still have to do business with the prevailing culture.

The unaccepted, split-off parts of the self, unintegrated with the current ego structure, form emotionally heightened complexes (Jung, 1934) which operate autonomously, in their raw, narcissistically sensitive form; by this I mean, with heightened feeling, reactiveness and self-preoccupation. I understand these 'narcissistic' reactions to be co-extensive with trauma (in other words, a trauma is a narcissistic wound). A traumatic experience is, by definition, one that the ego has not been able to bear nor therefore integrate at that particular time (see van der Kolk et al., 1996 or West, 2016).

Therefore, through lived experience, the individual develops an ego structure which is an adaptation to their relational environment in the form of unconsciously held and autonomously operating internal working models (Bowlby, 1969). These manifest in various ways, both as our everyday ego orientation, and as our specific relational forms and ways of engaging with others that Jung called the persona (Jung, 1951). As the ego develops and we become able to reflect on ourselves, what the neuroscientist Antonio Damasio calls 'extended consciousness' emerges, and we are able to form an 'autobiographical sense of self' over and above our moment-by-moment experience (this latter is our 'core consciousness') (see Damasio, 1999). I will quote from Daniel Stern at length here about this issue:

> During the second year of an infant's life language emerges, and in the process the senses of self and other acquire new attributes. Language ... makes parts of our known experience more shareable with others. In addition, it permits two people to create mutual experience of meaning that had been unknown before and could never have existed until fashioned by words. It also finally permits the child to begin to construct a narrative of his own life.

However, he continues:

> But in fact language is a double-edged sword. It also makes some parts of our experience less shareable with ourselves and others. It drives a wedge between two simultaneous forms of interpersonal experience: as it is lived and as it is verbally represented. Experience in the domains of emergent, core- and intersubjective relatedness, which continue irrespective of language, can be embraced only very partially in the domain of verbal

relatedness. And to the extent that events in the domain of verbal relatedness are held to be what has really happened, experiences in these other domains suffer an alienation. (They can become nether domains of experience). Language, then, causes a split in the experience of self. It also moves relatedness onto the impersonal, abstract level intrinsic to language and away from the personal, immediate level intrinsic to the other domains of relatedness.

(Stern 1985/1998, pp. 162–163)

So, in addition to the specific process of socialisation, where parts of the self that are not met are dissociated, the development of language adds a further layer of 'alienation', to use Stern's term, from lived experience and thus also from who we most truly are. In addition, the linguistic terms we use to describe things carry a further, implicit level of alienation and socialisation; for example, in the ways that any particular experience is named (or not named) and construed, including, sometimes, an implicit value judgement—see, for example, Foucault (1988) on what is considered 'mad'.

The process of the development of the self—individuation—is precisely the process of reclaiming both those rejected and undeveloped aspects of the personality—the individual's particular shadow (Jung, 1951)—as well as coming to learn to listen to and live by the ineffable, non-verbal, inchoate source from which they emerge—the Self.

The Relational Element

The process of analysis is significantly a joint process of developing a narrative which can embrace these other, disavowed parts of the self. The process is joint because any narrative will inevitably be born of the contribution of both analyst and patient to the verbal and non-verbal 'dialogue', and also because, on a deeper level, in order to come into being, the self needs to be met and accepted by an 'other'. Yet this other needs, at times, to be one who can closely, empathically, mirror the self. Thus the analyst can only truly meet in the other what they can accept and know in themselves, so that they can therefore be both 'as-self' and other to the patient at the same time.

However, any narrative is always only an approximation, as the self is always being born anew with each fresh moment of experience. It is the flow of experience that is the essential thing, and 'not knowing' takes us closer to the real realm of experience, unencumbered by both the verbal layer and historic ego-structures (see also Bion, 1970, ch. 4 or Fordham, 1993).

That said, the ego and its cognitive functioning, which builds and constitutes the autobiographical self, is a necessary container for the personality, giving a sense of self over and above the particular moment, and thus affording the person continuity and stability. However, the ego does need to be flexible and continue to develop so as to come to reflect the full nature of the individual as closely as possible; for example, as I once put it, 'the not-I is also who I am' (West, 2008).

To repeat my key point here—the unintegrated parts of the self require acceptance by an other in order to come into being and to be integrated into the personality. This is true for the developing infant, as well as for the dissociated parts of the self—the complexes—in adults. That acceptance needs to reach beyond the verbal domain, for example, that of pre-existing knowledge, and requires an openness to, and recognition of, new and emergent experience *in both the patient and the analyst*; this cannot simply be about theory learnt from a book.

When the opposition to the development of the self has been profound, for example, due to having been brought up by narcissistic, controlling, abusive or overly socialising caregivers, the individual may often oppose the otherness of the analyst in the analytic relationship and require particularly close identification at all times. This can readily be dismissed as the patient's pathological, 'narcissistic', 'anti-social' need for sameness, born of mistrust, or as a defence of the self (Fordham, 1974).

Should the analyst consistently oppose the patient's mistrust, and resolutely present the patient with their otherness (perhaps in an (unconscious?) attempt to further 'socialise' the patient), 'the baby may be lost with the bathwater', and the patient's unique self and experience, which requires the analyst's close identification, may be quashed. One of Michael Fordham's patients, who came to be known as 'K' and who exemplified what Fordham called defences of the self, has written about his experience of analysis and described how he could not bear to be 'translated' by Fordham's (verbal) interpretations (see 'K', 2007, 2008, 2014).

The core ethic of Jungian practice, as I understand it, is this acceptance of the patient (see the quote from Jung above on cultivating each part of our psyche, even when it is apparently unwanted), and the analyst's engagement with them. In the same paper Jung wrote:

> the therapeutic effect comes from the doctor's efforts to enter into the psyche of the patient, thus establishing a psychologically adapted relationship. For the patient is suffering precisely from the absence of such a relationship ... The transference is the patient's attempts to get into psychological rapport with the doctor. He needs this relationship if he is to overcome his dissociation.
>
> (Jung, 1921/1928, paras. 276–7)

And, significantly, regarding the analytic attitude, Jung continues:

> How can the patient learn to abandon his neurotic subterfuges when he sees the doctor playing hide-and-seek with his own personality, as though unable, for fear of being thought inferior, to drop the professional mask

of authority, competence, superior knowledge etc.? The touchstone of every analysis that has not stopped short at partial success, or come to a standstill with no success at all, is always this person-to-person relationship, a psychological situation where the patient confronts the doctor upon equal terms.

(Jung, 1921/1928, paras. 288–9)

Both Jung and, later, Heinz Kohut, realised that the emergence of new parts of the self are often accompanied by inflated states (e.g., Jung, 1946, para. 522), and that elements of idealisation, love and omnipotent thinking are inevitable, transitory experiences in the development of the personality (Kohut, 1971). Jung also described the 'mana personality' where the person becomes somewhat inflated and perhaps charismatic for a period of their development (Jung 1928, paras. 374–406; Lemos, 2020).

These inflationary experiences are inevitable, particularly in the process of addressing early narcissistic wounding, where the core parts of the self that have been dissociated continue their existence in 'primitive' form; for example, the hypersensitivity I mentioned earlier, where that part has never yet been accepted and brought into relationship. In other words, the person will be particularly sensitive to whether these parts of the self are acceptable to the analyst as they have not hitherto found a relationship in which they were accepted or where the person themselves felt able to express them.

I understand therefore, that the analyst's role is to meet with, accept and find a place and meaning for the patient's 'spontaneous gestures' (Winnicott, 1960). This is even when that behaviour might need to be challenged at some point by bringing the analyst's own self into the relationship; for example, pointing out (and subsequently exploring) the way that the patient may be dismissing the analyst's comments out of hand, or finding them universally critical.

Humility and the Move from Ego to Self

My overarching point here is that this turning inward, as part of the process of analysis, allows the development of the ego as it comes to encompass a greater breadth and depth of self-states, consonant with our humanness. This naturally entails coming to recognise the limits of the ego's ability to control both the world, others and the self, whilst coming to exercise a realistic agency. It will inevitably entail recognising and accepting our vulnerability, our openness to being affected by others and our reactions to being dysregulated. It will also encompass our developing sense of agency and ability to affect others, as well as our capacity to be playful, loving, hurtful or hateful.

Importantly, in this process of self-exploration, we usually, naturally develop humility as we discover that much of our wisdom and processing goes on unconsciously, outside of our ego's conscious control. We thus come to trust in this process and the broader, deeper Self (Jung, 1951). This is exemplified, for example, in dreaming, inspiration, creativity and intuition, or even in recognising that our basic feeling responses originate from outside of our control. There is then a development of self (in the ordinary sense of the word), as we discover that the centre of the self is beyond the ego.

There then tends to be a shift in the individual's centre of gravity so that they are living more open to, and 'from', the broader Self, rather than the ego. This development leads to states that are at the same time selfless (in the sense of being less driven by the ego construct), self-centred (in the sense of founded in and related to the true core of ourselves) and soulful (in the sense of being finely attuned, sensitive, connected and ineffable). I will say more about this below.

In this process we also come to recognise that 'we are who we humanly are', as broadly encompassed and expressed by the Self (all parts of the self and self-states), not 'simply' who we might like to be, as held narrowly by the ego. This amounts to having to come to work with, accept, and integrate what once lay in our shadow (Jung, 1951). This overall development is accompanied by a sense that we are coming to live in accord with our true self, not something we have constructed to fit in with our social milieu.

Whilst Freud did not recognise the wisdom of a Self beyond the ego, he described how the ego is instituted to adapt to the world and to pursue what is pleasurable and to avoid pain and distress. However, he recognised that through development we can come to embrace both suffering and joy, according to what is real. He understood this as a shift from the pleasure principle to the reality principle (Freud, 1920). This I see as encompassing some, but not all, of the phenomena related to the development of the ego–Self relationship that I am describing here. And by being 'oriented toward reality' I mean to emphasise the way that we are continuously, unconsciously processing what is going on in our environment and developing our relationship to it at a primitive, foundational, soul level (see Panksepp & Biven, 2013, p. 389 ff.; Solms & Panksepp, 2015). Our apparently 'unconscious' Self faces reality a lot more readily than our conscious ego may be prepared to do.

This process of the development of the ego and the shift toward the Self is not smooth, inevitable or even universal. The limiting factor is usually that the core of the self (in fact the part of the core self known as the protoself (Damasio, 1999, pp. 153–160)) is exquisitely sensitive, as it connects us to and is affected by both the relational and natural environments around us. The protoself, which is based in one of the foundational parts of the brain—the periaqueductal gray (PAG), seated in the brain stem—has one part that reacts toward pleasurable experiences and another that reacts against unpleasurable ones. In this way the psyche is all the time appraising (to use Bowlby's term) our experience in terms of good and bad, safe or dangerous, desirable and undesirable, and so on (see Solms & Turnbull, 2002, p. 108).

Whilst the ego has *some* control over how we navigate the world (agency), it is initially naturally averse to relinquishing that control in an attempt to avoid the suffering and distress that is, in fact, a natural consequence of human life. As I will now describe, such a limitation of contact with the core, and thus the full panoply of 'who we are', vitally truncates the deep connectedness with others, which could otherwise lead directly back to a deeper social engagement. To sum up what I am saying in this section, and to look somewhat ahead in my argument, our development requires that we are able to come to embrace suffering.

Loss of Contact with the Core/True Self

Paradoxically, I believe that the loss of contact with the core, and its potential deeper social engagement, occurs precisely through the process of socialisation in so far as that entails an alienation from parts of the self. The alternative would be a development of those parts by bringing them into relationship with the other. For example, this would be the difference between coming to learn through (painful) experience that our love, hatred, sexuality or aggression, or wish for care or touch are unacceptable or impossible, rather than that they are acceptable, accepted and a natural part of human life.

There is a necessary proviso here, namely that these expressions of self—love, hatred, sexuality, aggression, etc.—become acceptable if they are brought into relationship with an other who comes to be treated with respect as a separate person; or, as Jung (1917/1926/1943, para. 110 ff.) described, the archetypal expressions of self become humanised. Alternatively and additionally, we may need to be prepared to deal with the consequences of our self-expression if the other person, for particular reasons of their own, does not accept them. I am referring here to the need *not* to be strictly limited by the other person's personality, beliefs and prejudices as, to give an example, our self-expression might represent a challenge to the other's limited position or their wish to control us.

A clear example of what Jung calls the need to stand against the collective in the furtherance of individuation, would be where these beliefs and prejudices are 'simply' an embodiment of collective 'superego' values. This need to stand against the superego is discussed brilliantly in Loewald's (1979) paper on the Oedipal complex, in terms of the child's need to stand against, overthrow and surpass the father's limiting position in the furtherance of their own development; Ron Britton also discusses this need to stand against the superego (2003, ch. 7).

The Deeper Ethic of the Self

This raises the important question of the roots of our ethics and ways of behaving. Do we need sets of rules in order to tell us how to behave, and/or would we descend into anarchy, mayhem or rule by the most powerful, if such rules are challenged or overthrown? These are pressing issues, powerfully active in society at the moment, as individuals demand the right to live more truly according to the deepest callings of their souls, whether that is in relation to their sexuality, gender, race, nationality, creed or choice of partner. Many people across the globe are every day being killed for these expressions of their selves.

The shadow side of this movement is a willful self-centeredness that disregards and does not respect the other as a separate person of equal value in their own right. This goes to the heart of the tension between the rights of the individual to live true to themselves and the rights of others not to be unduly, adversely affected by what that means in practice. The articulation of these different positions with each other is the process by which culture develops.

It is this respect and valuing of the other that is both key to the deeper, natural, human ethic, *as well as emerging precisely from the deeper connection with the Self that I am describing in this chapter*. This ethic is best and most simply described in the ethic of Ubuntu, a Nguni Bantu term meaning 'humanity', which is sometimes translated as either, 'I am because you are' or 'I am because we are', or more generally, 'A person is a person through other persons'. As Desmond Tutu put it in his Templeton Prize interview:

> You cannot be human on your own ... we are only human through relationship ... [we live in] a blanket network of *inter*dependence; I need you in order for me to be me, and I need you to be you to the fullest ... we are made for complementarity.
>
> (Tutu, 2013)

Furthermore, as the quotation from Daniel Stern above makes clear, the development of the ego, concurrent with the development of language and our rational faculties, brings in a 'natural', inhibiting break from the 'vital' core of our being. This is presumably consequent upon the inhibitory, restraining, superego qualities (literally through a development of the forebrain) that humans developed in order to live in societies (Harari, 2015). However, the shadow side of this is that we can become alienated from our living, vital, ever-changing, vulnerable-yet-fierce self. Whilst the development of these cognitive functions (the ego) serves as an overarching protection and container for our vulnerable core, it can also readily alienate us from it.

This balance between self and other is achieved naturally through bringing parts of the self into relationship and their acceptance by the other. This occurs readily, although not without difficulty and struggle, in the process of analysis. Sometimes it may not occur at all if the analyst, for reasons unique to the individuals themselves and the dynamic of the analytic couple, blocks the patient's self-expression and thus individuation.

The Outward-Turning Process

And so, having reached the depths of the inward-turning process, there begins an outward-turning process as, in discovering the breadth and depths of our selves, we discover that we are intimately like others. We are thus able to both recognise and resonate with them and with their vulnerabilities and spirit. This occurs because, as I described above, the protoself is exquisitely sensitive and is intimately affected by the socio-cultural and natural environment around us.

This process works through identification, through the operation of mirror neurons (Gallese, 2001; Knox, 2011, ch. 3), so that when we observe someone doing something there is a mirror process within the protoself that allows us to 'know' what is going on. This is the process of empathy or, at this deep level, *participation mystique* (Jung, 1921/1928, para. 781; see also Winborn, 2014). Of course, we can be 'wrong' about how we interpret the other person's actions and intensions, perhaps interpreting defensively from within our own idiom or in order to protect the protoself from what feels like it would be threatening or unbearable experience. This can then be a potential opportunity for learning.

The process of development and individuation allows us to bear, encompass, appreciate and understand a greater range of self-states, within ourselves and others. It is a central part of the process of therapy to explore, develop and experience these states, and thus, in the process, both patient and analyst change and develop, as Jung describes (1946, para. 353 ff.).

In so far as we can allow ourselves to be open, including with the analyst, we establish an intimate connection with others, we *feel* connected, we feel that we belong, that we are part of humanity. We are moved by others and, at times, moved to engage with them, and, perhaps, moved to help, to offer care and support and, at times, to receive that in turn.

This could take myriad forms depending on our personality, experiences, skills and motivations and their particular foci. For example, it may be toward groups projects, working with individuals or working with the environment. It may equally be that the focus on the development of self has unforeseen and unforeseeable effects on others, some kind of trickle-down effect as Jung (1963) described, where others are affected by the change in us, in our personality, in the example we set, in our communications, or directly through our work, whether that is of an overtly therapeutic nature or not. At the most foundational level, because we are all interconnected through the protoself as I have described, when we change, others change/are influenced too.

This is a process that is not selfless, as in self-sacrificing, and certainly not motivated by wanting to look good in the eyes of others, but rather follows from a movement and motivation from within the Self. We are moved to engage with others and, through that shift of centre of gravity from the ego to the Self, it is selfless in that sense. I see this as essentially soulful—the action and connection of the soul. So, to repeat what I wrote earlier in this chapter, it is soulful, self-centred, and selfless at the same time.

The Inevitable Limitations of the Current Culture

These processes occur within our current culture, which is multifaceted and continually developing. All cultures develop idiosyncratically over the years and generations. Each particular culture and sub-culture, embodied by the many individuals encompassed by it, carries and models a variety of attitudes, values, mores and behaviours. Some of these are dominant, some get enshrined in laws, many continue at the margins, whilst some are actively opposed by the dominant culture.

There is, of course, a difference and sometimes an inherent dissonance and conflict between these different threads and streams. However, the dominant culture, usually though not always the one in government that is in control of law-making, sets the tone as to how inclusive or permissive the culture is of difference and dissonance, in short, how 'multicultural' it chooses to be.

However permissive, accepting and multicultural a culture is, human beings continue to develop and deepen their knowledge, experience and expression of their humanity, and this is rarely adequately reflected in the culture itself. There is always (hopefully) going to be a cutting edge where new attitudes emerge, embodying new forms of self-expression regarding, for example, security, attachment, power, economic organisation, gender, sexuality, behaviour, spiritual belief, meaning and purpose. Society as we know it will always naturally lag behind. As Jung (2009) pointed out, there is a tension and difference between the spirit of the times—the collective, social zeitgeist—and the spirit of the depths—our most personal as well as the deepest, most universal, human development. As Jung wrote of his very personal journey in *The Red Book*:

> I have learned that in addition to the spirit of this time there is still another spirit at work, namely that which rules the depths of everything contemporary. The spirit of this time would like to hear of use and value. I also thought this way, and my humanity still thinks this way. But that other spirit forces me nevertheless to speak, beyond justification, use, and meaning. Filled with human pride and blinded by the presumptuous spirit of the times, I long sought to hold that other spirit away from me. But I did not consider that the spirit of the depths from time immemorial and for all the future possesses a greater power than the spirit of this time, who changes with the generations. The spirit of the depths has subjugated all pride and arrogance to the power of judgment. He took away my belief in science, he robbed me of the joy of explaining and ordering things, and he let devotion to the ideals of this time die out in me. He forced me down to the last and simplest things.
>
> (Jung, 2009, p. 229)

The spirit of the depths continually brings forth that which is most important, 'the last and simplest things'. And this is as we struggle with the challenges set us by our particular social, political, economic, material and geographic location—is there enough food, how is it produced, how do we earn money to survive, live and thrive? How do we meet partners, fall in love, form relationships (if we choose to do so) and live fulfilling lives?

Our own personal development will inevitably sometimes be stifled by, although sometimes hopefully also assisted and supported by, these cultural attitudes, by the cultural complexes (Singer & Kimbles, 2004). When stifled, we must then stand against those cultural attitudes, with sometimes more, sometimes less conflict, difficulty, threat or loss involved. The more our core selves have been compromised, and the deeper from within us that the calling for wholeness originates, the more we might need to risk life or death in order to live according to the spirit of the depths.

In Conclusion

We sometimes need to turn away from and stand against the collective—whether that is embodied by the analyst, family members, other individuals, or society in general—precisely in so far as they embody the values and attitudes that have severed us from our true selves in the process of socialisation. The more we have been forced into having to comply, the more of ourselves will have experienced the violent dislocation of dissociation. A significant part of the work of analysis is to address this 'narcissistic wounding'.

However, as we begin to reclaim these lost parts, achieving a measure of wholeness, we are able to begin to live from our Self and to be more enlivened by the flow of energies. As we engage with others, our energies can then flow outward and enliven our relationships and the social worlds in which we engage and live. This is therefore a distinctly relational process, which requires an other to allow us to be ourselves, even whilst, at the beginning of the process, we turn against their otherness. In coming to live from our depths we discover both that we are connected to others, as well as discovering how much we have in common with them. With this depth of experience, and as a consequence of that more fully realised symmetry, we will naturally engage with others and will inevitably influence them, as we are influenced by them.

In this spirit I would like to end with an example, and specifically with a dream dreamt by Tom Singer (2019), which he describes and discusses in a paper he wrote on precisely this subject, entitled, 'The analyst as a citizen of the world'. The dream is as follows:

> I am attending a United Nations session and the discussion is focused on setting up a colossal cistern or water storage facility that will sit on top of the world. Whoever needs water in the world at a given time will be determined by a computer (this was long before computers were sitting on top of the world) – so that water for the whole earth will be regulated and distributed equitably. I thought to myself, 'I don't like computers

very much but maybe they could do a better job distributing water fairly than politicians have done'. It's a global watering hole ('whole' as I misspelled it in my dream book).

(Singer, 2019, p. 218)

I think this dream is a wonderful portrayal of the processes I have been describing, where the result of a growing 'wholeness' is access to the source of life/the waters of life/the libido. The 'computer' (the Self, always processing experience in the background/unconscious) can bypass the prejudices and power structures inherent in society/the ego (the politicians in the dream) and distribute those life energies where they are needed.

An individual who has deeply engaged with themselves in the ways I have described, and as Tom Singer exemplifies in his paper, will be more in touch with those life energies, not owning them for themselves but recognising that they come from outside our control (stored in the 'colossal cistern/water storage facility' that sits 'on top of the world'). These energies come by way of grace, from the Self, and life is enhanced, for self and others, by their expression. Thus a deeply personal journey results in the development of the deepest connection and communion with others.

One of the challenges of this journey, and perhaps the cutting edge and limiting factor, is that it puts us in touch with this most exquisitely sensitive part of our psyche (the protoself). Thus one aspect of the process of individuation is learning to bear, understand, value, live and work with these sensitivities and vulnerabilities—our multifaceted humanity—and take care of them within ourselves and others. Hopefully this can be achieved without attempting to control the world or to blame others for causing us distress, but rather accepting and participating in life as it is, with all its wonders and joys as well as its pain and suffering.

References

Bion, W.R. (1970). Opacity of Memory and Desire. *Attention and Interpretation: A Scientific Approach to Insight in Psycho-Analysis and Groups*, 2: 41–54.

Boston Change Process Study Group (BCPSG). (2010). *Change in Psychotherapy - A Unifying Paradigm*. W.W. Norton & Company.

Bowlby, J. (1969). *Attachment & Loss, Volume 1: Attachment*. Penguin Books.

Britton, R. (2003). *Sex, Death & the Superego - Experiences in Psychoanalysis*. Karnac.

Damasio, A. (1999). *The Feeling of What Happens: Body, Emotion and the Making of Consciousness*. Vintage.

Fordham, M. (1974). Defences of the Self. *Journal of Analytical Psychology*, 19: 192–199.

Fordham, M. (1993). On Not Knowing Beforehand. *Journal of Analytical Psychology*, 38: 127–136.

Foucault, M. (1988). *Madness and Civilization: A History of Insanity in the Age of Reason*. Vintage.

Freud, S. (1920). Beyond the Pleasure Principle. In *The Standard Edition of the Complete Psychological Works of Sigmund Freud, Vol. 18*: 1–64.

Gallese, V. (2001). The 'Shared Manifold' Hypothesis. *Journal of Consciousness Studies*, 8: 33–50.

Harari, Y.N. (2015). *Sapiens - A Brief History of Humankind*. Vintage.

Jung, C.G. (1917/1926/1943). On the Psychology of the Unconscious. In C.G. Jung, *Collected Works, Vol* 7. Routledge & Kegan Paul, 1958.

Jung, C.G. (1916/1964). Psychological Types. In C.G. Jung, *Collected Works, Vol*. 6. Routledge & Kegan Paul, 1958.

Jung, C.G. (1921/1928). The Therapeutic Value of Abreaction. In C.G. Jung, *Collected Works, Vol*. 16. Routledge & Kegan Paul, 1958.

Jung, C.G. (1928). The Relations between the Ego and the Unconscious. In C.G. Jung, *Collected Works, Vol*. 7. Routledge & Kegan Paul, 1958.

Jung, C.G. (1934). A Review of the Complex Theory. In C.G. Jung, *Collected Works, Vol*. 8. Routledge & Kegan Paul, 1958.

Jung, C.G. (1939). Conscious, Unconscious and Individuation. In C.G. Jung, *Collected Works, Vol*. 9i. Routledge & Kegan Paul, 1958.

Jung, C.G. (1946). The Psychology of the Transference. In C.G. Jung, *Collected Works, Vol*. 16. Routledge & Kegan Paul, 1958.

Jung, C.G. (1951). Aion: Researches into the Phenomenology of the Self. In C.G. Jung, *Collected Works, Vol*. 9ii. Routledge & Kegan Paul, 1958.

Jung, C.G. (1963). *Memories, Dreams, Reflections*. A. Jaffé (Ed.). Random House.

Jung, C.G. (2009). *The Red Book, Liber Novus*. W.W. Norton & Company.

'K'. (2007). 'What Works?' Response to the Paper by James Astor. *Journal of Analytical Psychology*, 52: 207–231.

'K'. (2008). Report from Borderland: An addendum to 'What Works'. *Journal of Analytical Psychology*, 53: 19–30.

'K'. (2014). On the Analysand's Need to Know the Real Person of the Analyst. *Journal of Analytical Psychology*, 59: 333–345.

Knox, J. (2011). *Self-Agency in Psychotherapy - Attachment, Autonomy and Intimacy*. W.W. Norton & Company.

Kohut, H. (1971). *The Analysis of the Self*. International University Press.

Lemos, P. (2020). The Glow of Telesphoros: A Brief Enquiry into the Sense of the Term 'Mana Personality' and the Dynamic of Experiences Behind It. *Journal of Analytical Psychology*, 65: 890–910.

Loewald, H.W. (1979). The Waning of the Oedipus Complex. *Journal of the American Psychoanalytic Association*, 27: 751–775.

Panksepp, J. & Biven, L. (2013). *The Archaeology of the Mind. Neuroevolutionary Origins of Human Emotions*. W.W. Norton & Company.

Porges, S.W. (2011). *The Polyvagal Theory: Neurophysiological Foundations of Emotions, Attachment, Communication, and Self-regulation*. W.W. Norton & Company.

Singer, T. (2019). The Analyst as a Citizen in the World. *Journal of Analytical Psychology*, 64: 206–224.

Singer, T. & Kimbles, S. (2004). *The Cultural Complex*. Routledge.

Solms, M. & Turnbull. O. (2002). *The Brain and the Inner World: An Introduction to the Neuroscience of Subjective Experience*. Other Press.

Solms, M. & Panksepp, J. (2015). *The Feeling Brain - Selected Papers on Neuropsychoanalysis*. Routledge.

Stern, D.N. (1985/1998). *The Interpersonal World of the Infant: A View from Psychoanalysis and Developmental Psychology.* Karnac.

Tronick. E.Z. (2007). *The Neurobehavioural and Social-Emotional Development of Infants and Children.* W.W. Norton & Company.

Tutu, D. (2013). youtube/0wZtfqZ271w

van der Kolk, B., McFarlane, A.C., & Weisaeth, L. (1996). *Traumatic Stress: The Effects of Overwhelming Experience on Mind, Body, and Society.* Guildford Press.

West, M. (2008). The Narrow Use of the Term Ego in Analytical Psychology: The "Not-I" is Also Who I Am. *Journal of Analytical Psychology,* 53: 367–388.

West, M. (2016). *Into the Darkest Places - Early Relational Trauma and Borderline States of Mind.* Karnac/Routledge.

Winborn, M. (2014). *Shared Realities - Participation Mystique and Beyond.* Fisher King Press.

Winnicott, D.W. (1960). Ego distortion in terms of True and False self. In: D.W. Winnicott, *The Maturational Processes and the Facilitating Environment: Studies in the Theory of Emotional Development.* Hogarth Press, 1965.

Chapter 7

The Intersubjective Perspective in Jung and Bion
Complementary Views of Unconscious Process, Structure, and Interaction

Mark Winborn

Jung's conception of the analytic process can be characterized from two primary perspectives: the intrapsychic (i.e., happening 'within' the 'individual') and the intersubjective. I propose that Jung's theoretical model gives preferential standing to the intrapsychic perspective, while the intersubjective perspective is more inferred and primarily described through Jung's use of the alchemical metaphor. In many respects, Jung's theoretical model, and how it is applied, often shifts between paradigms, i.e., containing themes from earlier positivist (Elkin, 1958; Hobson, 1971; Lichtenberg, 2004) or epistemological traditions as well as an implicit movement towards an intersubjective or ontological position. I also suggest that Bion's model of the psyche was one of the first psychoanalytic theories to formulate a model of psychological development and interaction that is based on intersubjective experience (which shares some commonalities, as well as differences, with the relational perspective).[1] In this chapter, I propose that Jung's mythopoetic model of the psyche and Bion's intersubjective perspective offer complementary theories of the psyche; forming, in Bion's language, a new psychoanalytic 'vertex' (Bion, 1970). Bion's model of the psyche is largely oriented around interactive processes rather than psychological structures (as in Jung's model), so it is well-suited for integration with Jung's theories (Winborn, 2018). Implications of a Jungian–Bionian hybrid clinical work are also discussed.

Intersubjectivity

During the 1980s a new movement in psychoanalysis, now referred to as the intersubjective perspective, began to emerge from the shifts in thinking and practice that grew out of the Kleinian, object relations, and Self Psychology perspectives. It was also influenced by the work of German philosophers Edmund Husserl, Jürgen Habermas, and Maurice Merleau-Ponty. Intersubjectivity emerged in reaction to the subject and object distinction that predominates in Western philosophy and science, often referred to as the positivist scientific orientation.[2] The intersubjective perspective in psychoanalysis moves from a one-person (isolated mind) perspective to a two-person

DOI: 10.4324/9781003429142-7

interactive field theory (Benjamin, 1990; Schwartz-Salant, 1995, 1998; Brown, 2010; Maier, 2014). This perspective also now widely incorporates Ogden's (1994a) concept of the 'analytic third' used to describe emergent experiences generated intersubjectively by the unique pairing of the analytic partners. The intersubjective position argues that the fundamental operation of mind is oriented towards connection and interaction, rather than discharge and gratification of instinctual pressures. Robert Stolorow, George Atwood, Donna Orange, Thomas Ogden, Jessica Benjamin, as well as post-Bionian writers such as Antonino Ferro, and Giuseppe Civitarese, are some of the influential contributors to the field (e.g. Atwood & Stolorow, 1979; Benjamin, 1990, 2004; Civitarese, 2008; Ferro, 2018; Ogden, 1991, 1994a, 1994b, 2019; Orange et. al., 1997; Stolorow et. al., 1994; Stolorow et.al., 2002).

Although the authors listed above share areas of conceptual overlap, there are several distinct lines of intersubjective theory that have developed. For example, an early intersubjective perspective emerged from Self Psychology and is foundationally associated with the work of Stolorow, Atwood, Brandchaft, and Orange. Benjamin utilizes the term in a manner that aligns more closely with the relational perspective. While Bion did not utilize the term intersubjective, many who have extended his work have located his theories within an intersubjective perspective (e.g. Baranger, 2012; Baranger & Baranger, 2008; Brown 2010). While I do not wish to minimize the important distinctions between the various schools of intersubjective theory, for the purpose of this chapter I will use the term in the broadest sense, i.e., that the analytic relationship is mutually created and influenced—consciously, unconsciously, and implicitly—by both patient and analyst.

The intersubjective model does not offer a new set of theories about psychological structures and processes such as complexes, id/ego/superego, or developmental stages. It provides a shift in focus from structures of the mind to the interactive process unfolding between two individuals which reveals elements of the subjective perspective of each individual as the process unfolds. Intersubjectivity theory (Atwood & Stolorow, 1979) holds that psychoanalysis is an intersubjective experience, i.e., that there are two subjectivities present which create an interactive, mutually created psychological field in which elements of the individual psyches cannot be clearly distinguished (Ogden, 1994b). This contrasts with the traditional Freudian view of the analytic dyad as being composed of two distinct and isolated psyches; what some intersubjectivists have come to term the myth of the isolated mind (Stolorow et al., 1994).

The distinction between earlier psychoanalytic models (intrapsychic) and the intersubjective model is sometimes referred to as the difference between a one-person psychology and a two-person psychology. The intrapsychic model is largely focused on what is occurring 'inside' the patient as a result of compromises between conflicting internal forces—such as the instinctual drives and the ego, or autonomous complexes and the ego complex. The traditional model of Freud depicts an inner world of drives and instinctually influenced unconscious fantasy. Freud's model refers primarily to processes assumed to originate within the patient which are projected onto the analyst who was typically depicted as a neutral observer and interpreter of such projections. Few analysts practicing today would identify with the stereotype of the detached observing analyst who interprets what is transpiring in the patient's mind from a position of analytic authority.

The intrapsychic mode of analysis, in both the Freudian and Jungian models, focuses on identifying various psychological structures and facilitating the withdrawal of those projected contents from the analyst (or other significant figures). The Jungian approach frequently involves a search for complexes and archetypal patterns in our patients. Such 'searching' can become an obstacle to the recognition of other experiences emerging in the analytic session. To some degree, the search for intrapsychic structures is at odds with the intersubjective perspective as described in the following passage by Ringstrom (2010, p. 200), who indicates that the intersubjective intent 'is to encourage clinicians to resist the reductionism and foreclosures common to the traditional psychoanalytic canon and to undauntingly pursue the closest iteration of subjective experience as possible', a subjective experience, he continues, 'that they adamantly aver can only be understood in the context that gives rise to it!' Quoting Orange (2003, p. 139), he concludes: 'Where these concepts are seen as a priori universal explanations of phenomena, the Intersubjectivists argue that, they can "lead us into believing that we know more than we do" ... and even worse, to go looking for it!'

Just as psychoanalytic theory has focused on the mother exclusively as the object of the infant's needs while ignoring the subjectivity of the mother, the intersubjectivist model argues that psychoanalysis in general has considered the analyst only as an object for the patient's projections and identifications, while neglecting the subjectivity of the analyst as the analyst is experienced by the patient. From the intersubjective position, the analyst's subjectivity is a significant contributor to the analytic situation.

In philosophy, the Archimedean point (*Punctum Archimedis*) is the hypothetical vantage point from which an observer can objectively perceive the subject of inquiry. As analytic therapy has progressed over the past 125 years, the field has progressively relinquished the Archimedean point of the analytic therapist as the detached, objective observer-commentator on the patient's neurotic conflicts. Jung, by proposing a model of analysis that places the analyst's personality at the center of the analytic process, anticipated aspects of the intersubjective development. In fact, Bovensiepen (2006, p. 457) places Jung's complex theory squarely within the intersubjective paradigm: 'I imagine then a complex to be a limited section, a sub-network from the entire fabric of intersubjective experiences.'

Because this intersubjective state is a co-created experience emerges from two subjectivities (patient and analyst) with their own narrative histories, defenses, and needs, the participants will have differing experiences of the intersubjective field, i.e. an asymmetrical intersubjectivity (Ogden, 1996; Stolorow et al., 1998; Grotstein, 2009). Although there is a shared subjectivity in the intersubjective understanding of the analytic encounter, the analytic relationship remains fundamentally asymmetrical because it takes place in an analytic setting, which is powerfully defined by the roles of analyst and analysand. Ogden (2004, p. 186) articulates the inherent and unavoidable asymmetry of the analytic dyad:

> As a result, the unconscious experience of the analysand is privileged in a specific way; i.e., it is the past and present experience of the analysand that is taken by the analytic pair as the principal (though not exclusive) subject of analytic discourse. The analyst's experience in and of the analytic third is (primarily) utilized as a vehicle for the understanding of the conscious and unconscious experience of the analysand.

In most analytic situations, it is likely that the analyst will have a greater depth of experience in working within the intersubjective field and, hopefully, has a greater awareness of how they respond in situations where mutually influential intersubjective forces are at work. Clearly, there has been a significant shift away from a model where the analyst possesses an objective perspective while the patient's perspective is subjective.

Intersubjective theory proposes that mental phenomena cannot be adequately understood if they are conceived of as a property that exists 'within' the patient's mind, conceptually isolated from the interactive matrix from which it emerges. Therefore, the patient's psychology is no longer seen moving the analysis forward in a particular direction, as it is perceived in more traditional psychoanalytic perspectives. In traditional psychoanalytic perspectives the analyst is seen as the facilitator but not the creator of the analytic focus. The intersubjective perspective sees the analyst as playing an active role in the creation of what emerges during the analytic process and in shaping the direction it takes. Intersubjective psychoanalysis proposes that all interactions should be considered contextually; interactions between the patient and analyst cannot be seen as separate from each other, but rather must be considered always as mutually influencing each other. This emphasis can be seen in the following passage from Stolorow (2011, p. 13): 'For us, intersubjective denotes neither a mode of experiencing nor a sharing of experience, but the contextual precondition for having any experience at all'. Benjamin (2004) indicates that we often conceptualize, experience, and discuss what happens between patient and analyst as a one-way street—the patient is described as the 'doer', and the analyst as the 'done to'. For example, descriptions of clinical work often contain language such as, *the patient was projecting their father complex onto me,* or *the patient, through projective identification, placed the abandoned child they did not want to acknowledge in themselves, into me causing me to feeling as though I was the abandoned child.* Benjamin argues we must move beyond the 'doer and done to' dynamic to fully understand what has emerged in the consulting room.

Intersubjective analysts see the clinician and the patient as unconsciously co-constructing the clinical experience from the interaction of both the analyst's and analysand's particular psychic qualities and subjective realities. They argue that the clinician's perceptions of the patient's psychology are always shaped by the clinician's subjectivity. Conversely, the patient's psychology is not conceptualized as something discoverable by an external, unbiased observer. In fact, intersubjectivity abandons the idea that the analyst can be a neutral, detached observer of the patient's psyche. Within this paradigm the observer and his language are inseparable from the observed, and the impact of the analyst and his organizing activity on the unfolding of the therapeutic relationship itself becomes a focus of analytic investigation and reflection. Therefore, the central metaphor of the intersubjective model is of a larger system or field in which experience is continually and mutually shaped by both the analytic participants. For example, according to Stolorow et al. (2002, pp. 109–110):

> Each participant in the inquiry has a perspective that gives access to a part or an aspect of reality. An infinite—or at least an indefinite—number of such perspectives is possible ... Since none of us can entirely escape the confines of our personal perspective, our view of truth is necessarily partial, but conversation can increase our access to the whole.

Intersubjectivity is a process theory which focuses on investigating and comprehending the intersubjective contexts in which psychological phenomena arise. In other words, the focus of the analyst is often less on the psychic contents of the patient emerging in the course of the analysis, and more on the process by which the analysis unfolds between the two participants and how that unfolding process impacts the analysand, the analyst, and the analytic dyad.

A main area in which the shift to an intersubjective position can be found is in the conceptualization of transference and countertransference (Benjamin, 2004). The shift outlined by the intersubjectivists reflects a change from the traditional view of psychoanalytic treatment as a series of techniques administered by the analyst for the purposes of imparting insight to the patient, towards a greater consideration of the experience and influence of the therapeutic interaction itself. Therefore, transference began to be viewed as the sum total of the patient's experience of the analyst (Little, 1957); not just the patient's patterns acquired in earlier life and projected onto the analyst, but also the emerging patterns co-created by analyst and patient. Rather than primarily associating the analyst's countertransference with misalignments to the patient due to the analyst's unresolved conflicts, the intersubjective perspective of countertransference includes all of the analyst's reactions to the patient, no matter what their source, allowing for greater recognition of the analyst's subjectivity in the analytic process.

Ontological and Epistemological Positions in Psychoanalysis

In a related manner, Ogden (2019) outlines two broad approaches to psycho-analysis: epistemological psychoanalysis and ontological psychoanalysis. As defined by Ogden, epistemological psychoanalysis concerns itself with know-ing, understanding, and explaining. He offers Freud and Melanie Klein as examples of epistemological approaches to psychoanalysis. Ontological psy-choanalysis concerns itself with the experience of being and becoming. Ogden points to Donald Winnicott and Wilfred Bion as examples of this approach. Ogden indicates that there is never a purely epistemological approach to any analysis just as there is never a purely ontological approach; the two approa-ches overlap and complement each other. However, an approach to analysis overly focused on the epistemological will likely prevent the ontological per-spective from entering the analytic experience.

Ogden indicates that this movement from an epistemological to an ontolo-gical approach within psychoanalysis has been occurring over the past seventy years. From Ogden's perspective, the ontological approach in Winni-cott is reflected in his shift from the symbolic meaning of play (as in Klein's work) to the experience of playing or the 'state of being' while at play. In other words, Klein observed the play of her child patients – attempting to decipher or understand the workings of their interior world through their play, whereas Winnicott was more focused on the child's experience of play and finding ways to enter into the play with them. Ogden (2019 p. 668) emphasizes Winnicott's concepts of 'transitional objects' and 'transitional spaces,' in which there is 'an intermediate state of experiencing, to which inner reality and external life both contribute,' as being particularly ontologi-cal in composition. Similarly, Bion shifts from an epistemological focus on the symbolic meaning of dreams (i.e., deciphering or understanding dreams) to the *experience* of dreaming in all its forms, whether sleeping or awake. Ogden indicates that Bion is principally an ontological thinker. The ontolo-gical approach is reflected in Bion's concept of analyst reverie, his attempt to be present in analysis 'without memory or desire' (Bion, 1967), and in his articulation of experience being created through the transformation of 'beta elements' (proto-experiences) into 'alpha elements' (represented bits of experience available for dreaming and waking-dreaming) through the 'alpha function' of the analyst (Bion, 1962/1983). Bion associates analytic reverie with the state of mind the mother has with her infant, allowing the infant's unspoken needs and experiences to occupy her mind and generate appropriate emotional and physical responses. He refers to this as the container/contained experience (Bion, 1993, p. 39) in which the infant is contained by the container formed in the mother's psyche. Ideally, the mother is also able to serve as container for her own intense emotions, such as anxiety, irritation, love, or hatred. Clearly, both reverie and container/contained experiences are framed within an ontological-intersubjective perspective. In Bion's model of psychological experience *being* supersedes *understanding*. For Bion, understanding remains useful to the analytic process only if it contributes to the further expansion of being.

Ogden does not locate Winnicott or Bion as belonging to the school of thought referred to as object relations theory (e.g., Klein, Fairbairn, and Guntrip). For object relations theorists, psychological growth involves understanding and freeing oneself from the persecutory, depressive, anxious, and dependent ties between internal objects and diminishing the influence of these internal objects on the ego. As Solomon (1991) points out, there are significant parallels between object relations theory and Jung's theory of complexes. Therefore, the effort by Analytical Psychologists to modify or de-potentiate complexes runs the same danger which Ogden (2019, pp. 673–674) identifies for object relations theory: i. e., the danger of falling into an epistemological approach to psyche while neglecting the ontological element of analysis, i.e., that of:

> Being and becoming more fully oneself, which to my mind, involves becoming more fully present and alive to one's thoughts, feelings and bodily states; becoming better able to sense one's own unique creative potentials and finding forms in which to develop them; feeling that one is speaking one's own ideas with a voice of one's own; becoming a larger person (perhaps more generous, more compassionate, more loving, more open) in one's relationships with others; developing more fully a humane and just value system and set of ethical standards; and so on.

In the passage above, many Jungians will perhaps note a parallel with Jung's process of individuation. Individuation is clearly an ontological concept which has broad overlap with Bion's ontological concept of 'coming into being' (Winborn, 2024).

To summarize, epistemological psychoanalysis principally involves the process of arriving at understandings of unconscious meaning. In contrast, the goal of ontological psychoanalysis is that of facilitating the patient's experience of creatively discovering meaning through experience and in that state of discovery, becoming more fully alive to experience. Jung's Analytical Psychology clearly has elements of both epistemological and ontological psychoanalysis. However, as it is often practiced and taught, the emphasis in Analytical Psychology remains focused on deciphering meaning, particularly in dreams, rather than holding a primary emphasis on experience. Hillman (1979) offers a more ontological approach to the analytic process when he proposed that our focus should be on the experience of image and soul rather than on translating dream images from 'night world' experience into 'day world' language.

Intersubjective Themes in Analytical Psychology

While there are several Jungian concepts which can be interpreted inter-subjectively or ontologically, I will explore only a few in this chapter. As mentioned earlier, Jung's Analytical Psychology has aspects of both the intrapsychic and intersubjective positions, for example, the metaphor of the alchemical bath, *participation mystique, coniunctio,* the wounded healer, his framing of transference in terms of alchemical states, and his concept of *synchronicity* can all be seen as precursory to the intersubjective position. Jung's utilization of alchemy as his primary device for describing these phenomena may make it difficult for those unfamiliar with his writing to grasp the essence of the underlying themes, but in his work on the concepts of the 'subtle body,' the 'psychoid realm,' and the '*coniunctio*' parallel concepts found in intersubjective psychoanalysis, such as the 'analytic third' and 'intersubjective field.' However, Jung does not move beyond using alchemy as a metaphor to describe qualities of the analytic process to explicate a theory of analytic interaction. In other words, unlike his theories of the unconscious, archetypes, or complexes, he never develops a conceptual framework based on his use of alchemical metaphor to articulate conceptual properties of the analytic field.

Precursory elements of the intersubjective perspective are anticipated in Jung's model of the analytic relationship, particularly in his discussion of the transference/countertransference matrix. However, in describing these concepts, Jung sometimes seems to use the concept intrapsychically at times and at other times intersubjectively.

The Analytic Third

According to Jung (1958), the transcendent function is a psychological function that arises from the tension between consciousness and the unconscious and supports the union of opposites. It expresses itself via the symbol and facilitates a transition from one psychological attitude or condition to another. In Jung's model, the transcendent function is the primary process by which individuation of the patient occurs. Jung describes the transcendent function as generating a new position; a new position which could be interpreted intrapsychically or intersubjectively:

> The shuttling to and from of arguments and affects represents the transcendent function of opposites. The confrontation of the two positions generates a tension charged with energy and creates a living third thing ... a movement out of the suspension between opposites, a living birth that leads to a new level of being, a new situation. The transcendent function manifests itself as a quality of conjoined opposites.
>
> (Jung, 1958, para. 189)

Jung's description of a 'living third thing' anticipates Ogden's (1994a, 1994b, 2004) concept of the 'analytic third.' Ogden conceptualizes along similar lines but makes a transition from the intrapsychic to the intersubjective, 'the author conceives of projective identification as a form of the analytic third in which the individual subjectivities of analyst and analysand are subjugated to a co-created third subject of analysis' (Ogden, 2004, p. 167). The analytic third is Ogden's conceptual term to refer to the intersubjectively-generated experience of the analytic pair. He sees the analytic third as unique to each analytic pair (analyst and analysand) and emerging from moment to moment in any given analytic session. The analytic third is the product of two subjectivities inter-acting resulting in a new experience emerging that is a novel product. For example, for Ogden, projective identification is not something done by the patient to the analyst, it is a unique reflection of the interaction of analyst and patient. This is different than the transcendent third proposed by Jung which is a new psychological position that emerges in an individual when there is sufficient tension held between two opposites.

Extending Jung's metaphor of an alchemical interactive field, Cwik (2011, 2017), drawing upon Jung's concept of active imagination, Ogden's concept of the analytic third (2004), and Bion's concept of reverie (1962/1983), proposes an intersubjective process he refers to as 'associative dreaming.' While Cwik con-ceptualizes associative dreaming as a reciprocally constellated analytic third which has implications for the analyst's countertransference, he also indicates that the focus of his concept extends beyond the transference/counter-transference matrix alone, indicating that emergent images, sensations, and memories also reflect, 'micro-activations of the transcendent function' (Cwik, 2011, p. 14). Using the illustration of a myth entering the analyst's mind during an analytic session, his focus is on an intuitive internal exploration of wondering how and why that particular myth entered the analyst's mind and what the myth says about the analytic field constellated between analyst and patient. Cwik goes on to describe how the analyst's 'associative dreaming' might then be introduced into the analytic exchange either implicitly or explicitly. Samuels (1989) describes a similar process but utilizes the metaphor of the *mundus imaginalis* (i.e, imaginal world), the analyst's embodied experience, and countertransference constella-tions. Samuels describes the *mundus imaginalis* as a shared dimension of experi-ence, similar to Winnicott's concept of 'transitional space' (Winnicott, 1971), Cwik's (2011) concept of associative dreaming, and Bion's concept of reverie (1962/1983). For Samuels, this shared experience is fundamentally an embodied experience which 'can be placed firmly *within* the imaginal real without *forget-ting* that there are two people present' (1989, p. 173, emphasis in original).

The Analytic Relationship

Jung clearly understood the mutually influencing aspects of the transference relationship and he saw those influences as being based, in large part, on the presence of *participation mystique* in the analytic relationship. He recognized early on that, 'It is not only the sufferer but the doctor as well, not only the object but also the subject' (Jung, 1929, para. 173) who is affected during analysis. His perspective on this, which goes beyond the unresolved or unexamined issues of the patient and the analyst, is captured most fully in *The Psychology of the Transference* which returns frequently to the image of the alchemical bath as a metaphor for the mutual unconscious influences of the analytic relationship. This reciprocal unconscious influence is also readily seen in Jung's diagram (1946, para. 422) of the analytic relationship, seen in Figure 7.1.

In this diagram Jung identifies the various levels or modes of interaction and influence between analyst and analysand, i.e. conscious to unconscious, and unconscious to unconscious.

Jung's conception of the analytic relationship was that it is mutually influential and interactive, often referring to it as a dialectical process (Beebe et al., 2001). He states this in various ways throughout his writing, often drawing upon analogies from alchemical writing, e.g., 'The meeting of two personalities is like the contact of two chemical substances: if there is any reaction, both are transformed'(Jung, 1933, p. 49). Jung did not believe the process could be transformative unless the analyst was 'in' the process with the patient:

> In any thoroughgoing analysis the whole personality of both patient and doctor is called into play. There are many cases which the doctor cannot cure without committing himself. When important matters are at stake, it makes all the difference whether the doctor sees himself as a part of the drama, or cloaks himself in his authority.
>
> (Jung, 1965, pp. 132–133).

Analytic Relationship

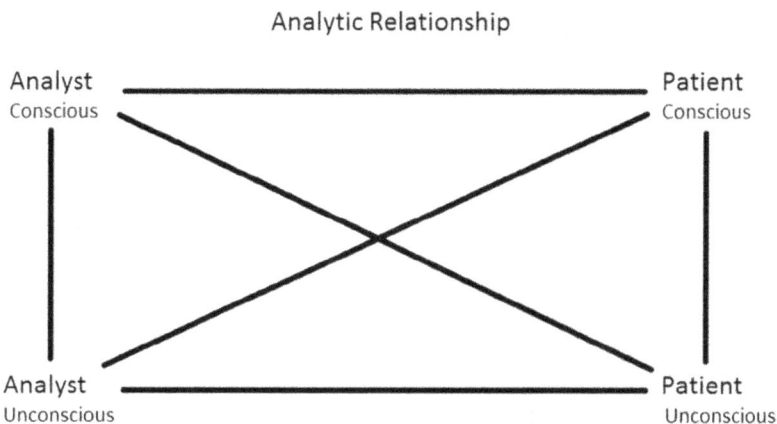

Figure 7.1

Another statement of this perspective follows:

> For two personalities to meet is like mixing two different chemical sub-
> stances: If there is any combination at all both are transformed. In any
> effective psychological treatment, the doctor is bound to influence the
> patient: But this influence can only take place if the patient has a reci-
> procal influence on the doctor. You can exert no influence if you are not
> susceptible to influence.
>
> (Jung, 1954/1966, para. 163)

Jung's conceptualization of the analytic dyad has been described as possessing
characteristics which anticipated the intersubjective perspective in psychoanalysis (Colman, 2007; Cwik, 2017; Schwartz-Salant, 1995). Jung's theories on
the nature of the analytic interaction can be seen as a precursory formulation of
the fundamental tenants of intersubjectivity and relational psychoanalysis.

Transference and Countertransference

Jung's longest treatise on the transference/countertransference matrix, *The
Psychology of the Transference* (1946), is based on an alchemical text first
published in 1550, the *Rosarium philosophorum*. Jung interprets the images
associated with the text, which depict various stages of transformation and
interaction, from a psychological and spiritual perspective. Jung felt that the
images portrayed in this alchemical text paralleled and informed the processes
he encountered in his sessions with analysands.

Jung focuses on the first 10 woodcuts from a series of 20 images. The
woodcuts and the accompanying text depict an incestuous love story between a
king and queen. The images portray an alchemical fountain or bath which
serves as the *vas hermeticum* to contain the various energies activated in their
interactions. The two figures move through various alchemical stages as the
woodcuts progress, dissolving and separation (*separatio* and *divisio*), joining of
opposites (*coniunctio*), blackening or darkening (*nigredo*), purification (*mundi-
ficatio*), and whitening or transformation (*albedo*). Jung utilized alchemy as a
metaphor for a variety of psychological processes, including the transference
and countertransference matrix. Samuels indicates that Jung's use of the
alchemical metaphor helps us bear in mind that 'the interpersonal and the
imaginal are equal partners and the technical implication is that content analysis and process analysis can, must coexist' (Samuels, 1989, p. 177).

Participation Mystique

The concept of *participation mystique* also illustrates the intersubjective
dimension in Jung's thinking (Winborn, 2014). Jung's most extensive discussion of the concept of participation mystique is found in his essay 'Archaic

Man' (1931). This essay outlines his ideas about the mental activity of indi-genous peoples,[3] i.e. that they function in a 'prelogical state of mind,' that they 'were simpler and more childlike,' and unpsychological by which he means that psychological experiences are perceived as occurring outside of the indigenous individual in an objective way. These inferences about the psychological experience of indigenous peoples underlie Jung's central notion of *participation mystique*—namely that in *participation mystique* experience there is a blurring of psychological boundaries between individuals, between individuals and their environment, and in some instance between individuals and objects. It is the blurring of subjectivities which aligns *participation mystique* with the intersubjective perspective.

A number of analytical psychologists, e.g. Gordon (1967), Davidson (1974), Samuels (1985), Schwartz-Salant (1988), Field (1991), and Wiener (2009), have highlighted the similarity between Jung's utilization of the participation mystique concept and the concept of projective identification, first proposed by Melanie Klein (1946), in which parts of the self and internal objects of the infant are split off and projected onto an external object. Thomson (2001, p. 385) highlights the intersubjective element inherent in *participation mystique*: 'Projective identification as a process of emergence from *participation mystique* reveals itself as a means of sharing understanding through non-verbal experience, where the verbalizations are at best approximations of the content of the analytic relationship.' Developing this point further, Wiener (2009, p. 54) ties together the overlapping concepts of, transference, projective identifi-cation, and intersubjectivity as well as highlighting the danger for the analytic process if these connections are not recognized: 'Research findings also sup-port a central role for projective identification (in Jung's language, *participa-tion mystique)* at the core of intersubjective relating. We cannot help but be affected by our patients, and, consequently, we ignore transference phenom-ena at our peril.'

Neumann (1989) provides an interpretation and extension of *participation mystique,* articulating the underlying dynamics in language even more closely aligned with the intersubjective perspective. His concept of unitary reality builds on Jung's work around the psychoid realm (the essentially indivisible connection between psyche and matter), *participation mystique*, synchronicity (the meaningful but non-causal relationship between events—often inner and outer events), the archetypal structure of experience, the *anima mundi* (world soul), the *unus mundus* (i.e. one world), and the *unio mentalis* (the unification of soul and spirit). Neumann's concept of unitary reality was originally pub-lished in the 1952 *Eranos Yearbook* and he can be considered, along with Jung, one of the first intersubjective theorists. His theory of unitary reality anticipates similar work on intersubjectivity by authors such as Atwood and Stolorow (1984), Ogden (1994b), and Benjamin (2004).

Neumann proposes that there are two types of consciousness: 'conscious knowledge' and 'perceiving knowledge' or 'extraneous knowledge'. He associates 'conscious knowledge' with the ego-complex which splits experience into polarized categories and indicates that 'perceiving' or 'extraneous' consciousness is knowledge that is beyond the ability of the ego-complex to process. It is through this 'extraneous knowledge dimension' which Neumann hypothesizes that a meaningful order and connection with our environments is discernible. Neumann argues that through the excess focus on conscious knowledge we have renounced awareness of the world's unity and continuity, as well as its aliveness and significance, which Neumann indicates is primarily experienced through feelings and intuition. Expanding on this idea, Neumann (1989, p. 98) indicates, 'We have lost our sense of unitary reality, our experience of identity and of the sympathy of all things, and as a result we have fallen into solitude and isolation of a dead and empty cosmic space.'

Neumann desires to resurrect the idea of *participation mystique* from being used as a label to characterize primitive forms of thinking, in which the distinction between subject and object is blurred, to one in which a specific type of knowledge which he refers to as 'field knowledge' is exchanged between one being and another existing within the same 'reality field.' Neumann indicates that inner and outer are merely categories of a conscious knowledge system, not reality itself. In the field of unitary reality, the distinction between inner and outer is diminished, psychical and physical are no longer opposites, and the boundaries of form defining a person or object can become blurred. Neumann (1989, p. 27) argues that when a personality is immersed in an archetypal field it means, 'There is a reciprocal co-ordination between world and psyche ... a co-ordination which is based on the archetypal structure which embraces both, or of which both are partial aspects ...' which 'leads to an emotionally toned unitary experience.' Neumann's description underscores the intersubjective and transpersonal (Tennes, 2007) nature of the field of unitary reality.

Knowing, Being Known, Knowing With

Another Jungian conceptualization which parallels the intersubjective position is Edinger's (1984) description of consciousness emerging through the interactive process of knowing and being known. Etymologically, consciousness derives from 'con' meaning 'with' or 'together' and 'scire' meaning 'to know' or 'to see.' Thus, consciousness means 'knowing with' or 'seeing with' an 'other.' Edinger indicates that there are three experiential facets of consciousness—*knowing, being known, and knowing with*. Edinger (1984, p. 54) cites the Christian mystic Meister Eckart to illustrate his position:

> It must be understood that this is all the same thing: knowing God and being known by God, and seeing God and being seen by God ... Even as the luminous air is not distinguishable from its luminant, for it is luminous with what illumines it, so do we know by being known.

Knowing refers to being the knowing subject. To know requires, first of all, that undifferentiated experience be split into subject and object, the knower and known. Edinger (1984, p. 37) indicates, 'This act of cognition, of conscious discrimination sunders the world into opposites, for experience of the world is only possible through opposites.' From the intersubjective position it is not possible to be the knowing subject without also being known by the object because the experience of being known constellates the self/subject.

Being known, Edinger continues, refers to being the known object: 'To achieve authentic consciousness the ego must ... go through the experience of being the object of knowledge, with the function of the knowing subject residing in the "other"' (1984, p. 41). In analysis, the analyst often carries the projection of the 'knowing other'.

Finally, Edinger describes *knowing with* as a function of Eros and reflecting a state of *coniunctio*. The experience of knowing with can be in relationship with an outer other (a person), or an inner other (the Self). According to Edinger, the process of becoming conscious requires both seeing and being seen, knowing and being known.

Intersubjective Themes in Bion

While Bion's work preceded the intersubjective turn, Bion can readily be conceptualized as fitting within the intersubjective perspective in psychoanalysis which began to emerge in the 1980s. Ogden (1994b) identifies Bion as a precursor to intersubjective theory, especially in Bion's development of the notion of projective identification as a means of communication.

Other precursors to the intersubjective perspective can also be discerned in Bion's (1990, pp. 4–5) work:

> Similarly in psycho-analysis: when approaching the unconscious—that is, what we do not know, not what we do know—we, patient and analyst alike, are certain to be disturbed. Anyone who is going to see a patient tomorrow should, at some point, experience fear. In every consulting room there ought to be two rather frightened people: the patient and the psycho-analyst. If they are not, one wonders why they are bothering to find out what everyone knows.

Theory of Thinking

In Bion's model, the process of psychological change or transformation occurs intersubjectively and experientially—what Bion (1962/1983) calls 'learning from experience.' and is conceptualized in his theory of thinking (Bion, 1993, pp. 110–119). Bion refers frequently to 'thinking' in his writing, but his idea of thinking is not synonymous with cognition or intellectual acts. He is using the word 'thinking' as a shorthand term for the capacity for being through reflective embodied experiencing of emotion. Hence, emotional experience is the foundation from which the capacity for increasingly complex forms of reflection emerges. In Bion's model there is no dichotomy or opposition between emotional experience and thinking in the way Jung refers to feeling and thinking as functions which are opposed in his theory of typology (Jung, 1971). Rather Bion sees emotional experience as an integral element of 'thinking'.

For Bion, the work of analysis still involves the work of understanding symbolic content which reveals unconscious meanings, but analysis also becomes a process of metabolizing un-symbolized aspects of experience which have never been conscious and never been repressed because they've never risen to the level of a 'thought.' Only by working at this level can those experiences become available for reflection and symbol production. Bion refers to these bits of un-symbolized experience as 'beta elements' (Bion 1962/1983). Because beta elements operate outside awareness and have not yet been represented, they are not available for thought, reflection, or learning and are not subject to repression or suppression.

Elements of experience which have become sufficiently coalesced to be reflected upon by the individual or in the presence of another person Bion refers to as 'alpha elements' (Bion 1962/1983). Alpha elements are produced from the impressions of experience which have been made storable and available for dream thoughts and for unconscious waking dream thought. Alpha elements become building blocks of experience which have the potential to become connected together to form dream thoughts. For Bion, 'dream thoughts' are the fundamental components of dreaming which he conceptualizes as occurring both during sleeping and waking states unless the capacity to dream has been disrupted.

'Alpha function' is the intersubjective psychological process by which beta elements become transformed into alpha elements. Analytically this refers to the capacity of the analyst to contain elements of the patient's psyche while engaging in reverie about the beta elements of the patient to facilitate their transformation into alpha elements. For the patient to learn from experience the alpha function of the analyst must operate on the awareness of the unrepresented emotional proto-experiences of the patient until the patient develops sufficient alpha function to participate in the process as a intersubjectively constellated alpha function.

Bion's concept of alpha function is similar to Jung's (1958) concept of the transcendent function except in Jung's model the transcendent function operates to generate symbolic material and functions intrapsychically while the alpha function operates intersubjectively and on the level of the pre-representational. We can think of alpha function as operating on a more fundamental level of transformation than the transcendent function – the level of very discrete, almost imperceptible shifts which transform undigested elements of experience into usable bits of experience. These transformed bits become the building blocks of larger shifts involved with the symbolization process of the transcendent function and the capacity to live into individuation. It seems likely that the alpha function and the transcendent function of the analyst work in conjunction but are engaged with transforming different levels of experience. Or as Cwik (2011, p. 31) indicates, these small transformative experiences reflect 'micro-activations of the transcendent function resulting in new images, thoughts, and feelings that appear to the analyst.' Civitarese and Ferro (2013, p. 200) and Grotstein (2007, p. 271), conceptualizing along similar lines, propose an 'alpha-megafunction' operating on a similar level of experience as Jung's transcendent function.

The Selected Fact

From many possible sources arising in an analytic session, the analyst must temporarily narrow their focus for an interpretation to emerge. Bion (1962/1983, 1992) referred to this narrowing of focus as the emergence of 'the selected fact.' The selected fact is a transitory area of focus around an emotional experience from which an interpretation is likely to be formed. Bion is not making a statement about the accuracy of an observation or a statement of absolute truth by electing to use the word 'fact.' Instead, he is referring to a sense of emotional immediacy (or absence of emotional experience) that crystalizes some aspect of the patient's psychic reality or the shared experience of the analyst and analysand. From the perspective of the intersubjective field, the selected fact (we could also refer to 'the selected scene' or 'the selected character') is a product of the field rather than emerging solely from the analyst or the analysand. In many ways, the selected fact has correspondence with the Jungian concept of symbol, but the function of the selected fact is less specific in Bion's model than the concept of symbol in Jung's model and is conceived of as emanating from the field rather than being generated by the transcendent function of the patient.

Working from a Hybrid Jungian-Bionian Model

My work as a Jungian psychoanalyst revolves around the developmental perspective in Analytical Psychology. I have also been deeply influenced by the work of Wilfred Bion and consider my orientation to be a hybrid of the Jungian and Bionian models. Despite conceptual and linguistic divergences, Bion and Jung focus their work along several similar lines—e.g. an emphasis on psychic reality, transcendent aspects of the psyche and experience, and the mutuality of influence in the analytic situation. Sullivan (2012, pp. 689–690) nicely summarizes the relationship between Bion's opus and that of Jung:

> I believe that it is the late Bion whose ideas regarding O, doubt, Faith, the impossibility of Knowing and the consequent need to focus instead on moving-toward-knowing, on endlessly becoming rather than existing in a fixed shape is the Bion whose ideas can be thought of as "Jungian" in nature ... Analysts like Ferro, Grotstein and the Symingtons see Bion's later work as bringing us to a new kind of analysis ... For this Jungian, the late Bion is a brilliant expander of Jung's perspective.

Working from a Jungian-Bionian perspective I recognize the existence and importance of both the internal drama and the intersubjective matrix. They coexist and interpenetrate. It is not a question of one or the other. The analyst and analysand both reside in a *vas hermeticum* and are both subject to the alchemical processes occurring in the *vas*—conscious and unconscious, implicit and explicit, interpersonal and intrapsychic, and of course, transpersonal. While the universals of human experience expressed through Jung's archetypal theory motivated my initial involvement with Analytical Psychology, over the years I've become more focused on the specificity and uniqueness of the individual and the narrative they are living out, as well as the uniqueness of each analytic dyad. As Gabbard and Ogden (2009, p. 322) state: 'With each patient, we have the responsibility to become an analyst whom we have never been before.' My attention has shifted from a primary focus on projection, symbol, complex, and archetype to a more experientially focused intersubjective stance.

This perspective involves allowing the patient to utilize the faculties of the analyst's psyche, i.e. to borrow the analyst's reflective capacity, symbolic attitude, capacity to hold the tension of opposites, and transcendent function. In the Bionian model this also involves the utilization of the analyst's alpha function. As part of this process the analyst must create a space to reflect on their experience, the experience of the patient, and the qualities of the field emerging in the consulting room, i.e. the analytic reverie. Ideally, through this process, the analysand can come to think about, reflect on, and experience themselves. This initially occurs unconsciously but hopefully it becomes internalized as a conscious process as well. Working from this perspective requires the analyst to process and digest their own thoughts, feelings, fantasies, and sensations while at the same time doing the same with the patient's experience. Not all of the information needed for an analysis will come from the patient. Often the material emerging from the analyst's subjective experience will be as crucial in understanding the patient as what the patient says or what is revealed in their dreams.

From this Jungian-Bionian hybrid model, the role of interpretation as a transformational action operates in tandem with the transformative potential of the analytic relationship and the intersubjective experience. Doctors (2009, p. 462) proposes that interpretation is itself an intersubjective process:

Any understanding achieved is a joint creation, emerging from the inter-action, rather than an objective truth about one person discovered by another. Interpretations not only emerge from the interaction, but also recursively influence the relationship, for better or worse. In this ongoing reverberatory process, it is often useful to weave into interpretive activity one's sense of where the patient is and where the analyst is at any given intersubjective moment.

There is a shift away from a one-person psychological model in which the analyst interprets from the stance of a knowing observer of the patient's mind. The analytic process becomes centered on a two-person intersubjective experience of recognition and being recognized, knowing and being known. As Benjamin (1990, p. 35) puts it:

> [T]he other must be recognized as another subject in order for the self to fully experience his or her subjectivity in the other's presence. This means that we have a need for recognition and that we have a capacity to recognize others in return, thus making mutual recognition possible.

Bion's work, especially his focus on unrepresented states (which Bion refers to as beta elements), provides a means of engaging a layer of experience com-monly encountered with our analysands, but which is not made explicit in the Jungian model (Winborn, 2017). Blending Bion's conceptual model with my Jungian background has also provided a model for working with analysands who have limited or disrupted symbolic capacity (Winborn, 2023). Finally, Bion's approach to psychological experience has deepened my sensitivity to the subtle, ephemeral elements of the interactive field (Winborn, 2022). Integrating a Bionian-intersubjective-ontological perspective with my Jungian foundation has deepened my capacity to 'learn from experience' (Bion, 1962/1983). Learning from experience is the capacity to make linkages between elements of experience—such as thoughts, feelings, bodily sensations, or sensory impres-sions—allowing these elements to be digested, integrated, and imaged so that they become part of the fabric of who I am—as a person and an analyst.

Notes

1 For example, according to Ringstrom (2002, p. 198) a primary commonality "… is that their clinical methodology shares an empathic/introspective/interpretive tradi-tion. That is, the patient's subjective experience is approached, at least initially with a great deal of empathic inquiry, while the analyst also introspects about her own cornucopia of theories and experiences in her attempt to better understand her patient's experience as well as to better understand her limitations in understanding. Finally, the result of empathic/introspective inquiry hopefully produces provisional interpretations about the meaning of the patient's experience; interpretations, that link his past, his present and configure his anticipation of his future."

2 A fundamental goal of positivist inquiry is to generate explanatory associations or causal relationships that ultimately lead to prediction and control of the phenomena in question.

3 Jung typically referred to such groups as 'primitives' reflecting the colonialist mindset of the time.

References

Atwood, G. & Stolorow, R. (1979). *Faces in a cloud: Intersubjectivity and personality theory.* Aronson.

Atwood, G. & Stolorow, R. (1984). *Structures of subjectivity: Explorations in psychoanalytic phenomenology.* Analytic Press.

Baranger, M. (2012). The intrapsychic and the intersubjective in contemporary psychoanalysis. *International Forum of Psychoanalysis,* 21: 130–135.

Baranger, M. & Baranger, W. (2008). The analytic situation as a dynamic field. *Inter. J. of Psycho-Anal.,* 89: 795–826.

Benjamin, J. (1990). An outline of intersubjectivity. *Psychoanalytic Psychology,* 7S (supplement): 33–46.

Benjamin, J. (2004). Beyond doer and done to. *Psychoanal. Q.,* 73(1): 5–46.

Bion, W.R. (1962/1983). *Learning from experience.* Aronson.

Bion W.R. (1967). Notes on memory and desire. *Psychoanal. Forum,* 2: 272–280.

Bion, W. R. (1970). *Attention and interpretation.* Karnac.

Bion, W.R. (1990). *Brazilian seminars.* Karnac.

Bion, W.R. (1992). *Cogitations.* Karnac.

Bion, W.R. (1993). *Second thoughts.* Karnac.

Bovensiepen, G. (2006). Attachment-dissociation network: Some thoughts about a modern complex theory. *J. Anal. Psychol.,* 51: 451–466.

Brown, L. J. (2010). Klein, Bion, and intersubjectivity: Becoming, transforming, and dreaming. *Psychoanalytic Dialogues,* 20: 669–682.

Civitarese, G. (2008). *The intimate room: Theory and technique of the analytic field.* Routledge.

Civitarese, G. & Ferro, A. (2013). The meaning and use of metaphor in analytic field theory. *Psychoanalytic Inquiry,* 33: 190–209.

Colman, W. (2007). Symbolic conceptions: The idea of the third. *J. Anal. Psychol.,* 52: 565–583.

Cwik, A.J. (2011). Associative dreaming: Reverie and active imagination. *J. Anal. Psychol.,* 56: 14–36.

Cwik, A.J. (2017). What is a Jungian analyst dreaming when myth comes to mind? Thirdness as an aspect of the anima media natura. *J. Anal. Psychol.,* 62: 107–129.

Davidson, D. (1974). Invasion and separation. In M. Fordham (Ed.), *Analytical psychology: A modern science,* (pp. 162–172). Karnac.

Doctors, S.R. (2009). Interpretation as a relational process. *Int. J. Psychoanal. Self Psychol.,* 4: 449–465.

Edinger, E. (1984). *The creation of consciousness.* Inner-City Books.

Elkin, H. (1958). On the origin of the self. *Psychoanalytic Rev.,* 45: 57–76.

Ferro, A. (2018). *Contemporary Bionian theory and technique.* Routledge.

Field, N. (1991). Projective identification: Mechanism or mystery? *J. Anal. Psychol.,* 36: 93–109.

Gabbard, G.O. and Ogden, T.H. (2009). On becoming a psychoanalyst. *Int. J. Psycho-Anal.*, 90(2): 311–327.

Gordon, R. (1967). Symbols: Content and process, *J. Anal. Psychol.*, 12: 23–34.

Groesbeck, C.J. (1975). The archetypal image of the wounded healer. *J. Anal. Psychol.*, 20:122–145.

Grotstein, J. (2007). *A beam of intense darkness: Wilfred Bion's legacy to psychoanalysis.* Routledge.

Grotstein, J. (2009). *But at the same time and on another level. Vol. 1.* Karnac.

Hillman, J. (1979). *The dream and the underworld.* Harper & Row.

Hobson, R. F. (1971). Imagination and amplification in psychotherapy. *J. Anal. Psychol.*, 16: 79–105.

Jung, C.G. (1929). Problems of modern psychotherapy. In *Collected works, Vol. 16* (1954/1966, pp. 53–75). Princeton University Press.

Jung, C.G. (1931). Archaic man. In *Collected works, Vol. 10* (1964/1970, pp. 50–73). Princeton University Press.

Jung, C.G. (1933). *Modern man in search of a soul.* Harcourt Brace Jovanovich.

Jung, C.G. (1946). The psychology of the transference. In *Collected works, Vol. 16* (1954/1966, pp. 163–323). Princeton University Press.

Jung, C.G. (1954/1966). *Collected works, Vol. 16: The practice of psychotherapy.* Princeton University Press.

Jung, C.G. (1958). The transcendent function. In *Collected works, Vol. 8* (1960/1969, pp. 67–91). Princeton University Press.

Jung, C.G. (1965). *Memories, dreams, reflections.* Vintage.

Jung, C.G. (1971). *Collected works, Vol. 6: Psychological types.* Princeton University Press.

Klein, M. (1946). Notes on some schizoid mechanisms. *Int. J. Psycho-Anal.*, 27: 99–110.

Lichtenberg, J. (2004). Experience and inference: How far will science carry us? *J. Anal. Psychol.*, 49: 133–142.

Little, M. (1957). 'R' — the analyst's total response to his patient's needs. *Int. J. Psychoanal.*, 38: 240–254.

Maier, C. (2014). Intersubjectivity and the creation of meaning in the analytic process. *J. Anal. Psychol.*, 59: 624–640.

Neumann, E. (1989). *The place of creation.* Princeton University Press.

Ogden, T. H. (1991). Analysing the matrix of transference. *Int. J. Psychoanal.*, 72: 593–605.

Ogden T.H. (1994a). The analytic third. Working with intersubjective clinical facts. *Int. J. Psychoanal.*, 75: 3–20.

Ogden, T.H. (1994b). *Subjects of analysis.* Jason Aronson.

Ogden, T.H. (1996). Reconsidering three aspects of psychoanalytic technique. *Int. J. Psychoanal.*, 77: 883–899.

Ogden, T.H. (2004). The analytic third: Implications for psychoanalytic theory and technique. *Psychoanal. Q.*, 73(1): 167–195.

Ogden, T. H. (2019). Ontological psychoanalysis or "What do you want to be when you grow up?" *Psychoanalytic Quarterly*, 88: 661–684.

Orange, D. (2003). Do we really all know? Reply to commentary. *Psychoanalytic Dialogues*, 13: 129–140.

Orange, D., Atwood, G., & Stolorow, R. (1997). *Working intersubjectively: Contextualism in psychoanalytic practice.* The Analytic Press.

Ringstrom, P.A. (2010). Meeting Mitchell's challenge: A comparison of relational psy-choanalysis and intersubjective systems theory. *Psychoanalytic Dialogues*, 20: 196–218.

Samuels, A. (1985). *Jung and the post-Jungians*. Routledge.

Samuels, A. (1989). *The plural psyche: Personality, morality and the father*. Routledge.

Schwartz-Salant, N. (1988). Archetypal foundations of projective identification. *J. Anal. Psychol.*, 33: 39–64.

Schwartz-Salant, N. (1995). On the interactive field as the analytic object. In M. Stein, (Ed.) *The interactive field in analysis* (pp. 1–36). Chiron.

Schwartz-Salant, N. (1998). *The mystery of human relationship: Alchemy and the transformation of the self*. Routledge.

Sedgwick, D. (1994). *The wounded healer: Countertransference from a Jungian per-spective*. Routledge.

Solomon, H.M. (1991). Archetypal psychology and object relations theory. *J. Anal. Psychol.*, 36(3): 307–329.

Stolorow, R.D. (2011). From mind to world, from drive to affectivity: A phenomen-ological-contextualist psychoanalytic perspective. *Attachment: New Directions in Relational Psychoanalysis and Psychotherapy*, 5: 1–14.

Stolorow, R., Atwood, G. & Brandchaft, B. (Eds.) (1994). *The intersubjective perspec-tive*. Aronson/Rowman & Littlefield.

Stolorow, R., Orange, D. & Atwood, G. (1998). Projective identification begone!: Commentary on paper by Susan H. Sands. *Psychoanalytic Dialogues*, 8: 719–772.

Stolorow, R., Orange, D. & Atwood, G. (2002). *Worlds of experience: Interweaving philosophical and clinical dimensions in psychoanalysis*. Basic Books.

Sullivan, B.S. (2012). Review of Mawson, Chris (Ed.). Bion Today. London and New York: Routledge, 2011. *J. Anal. Psychol.*, 57: 688–690.

Tennes, M. (2007). Beyond intersubjectivity: The transpersonal dimension of the psy-choanalytic encounter. *Contemporary Psychoanalysis*, 43: 505–525.

Thomson, J. (2001). Review of Roger Brooke (Ed.) Pathways into the Jungian world: phenomenology and analytical psychology. *J. Anal. Psychol.*, 46: 384–387.

Wiener, J. (2009). *The therapeutic relationship: Transference, countertransference, and the making of meaning*. Texas A&M Univ. Press.

Winborn, M. (Ed.) (2014). *Shared realities: Participation mystique and beyond*. Fisher King Press.

Winborn, M. (2017). The colorless canvas: Non-representational states and implications for analytical psychology. In *Anima Mundi in transition: Cultural, clinical and profes-sional challenges - proceedings of the 20th IAAP Congress – Kyoto (*pp. 430–439). Daimon Verlag.

Winborn, M. (2018). Jung and Bion: Intersecting vertices. In R.S. Brown (Ed.), *Re-encountering Jung: Analytical psychology and contemporary psychoanalysis* (pp. 85–111). Routledge.

Winborn, M. (2022). Whispering at the edges: Engaging ephemeral phenomena. *J. Anal. Psychol.*, 67(1): 363–374.

Winborn, M. (2023). Working with patients with disruptions in symbolic capacity. *J. Anal. Psychol.*, 68(1): 87–108.

Winborn, M. (2024). Coming into being: Telos in Jung and Bion, In G. Amundson (Ed), *A Jungian study of the teleology of psychic reality: Psychological and philoso-phical perspectives on the concept of future-orientation* (pp. 24–57). Routledge.

Winnicott, D.W. (1971). *Playing and reality*. Routledge.

Index

For Product Safety Concerns and Information please contact our EU
representative GPSR@taylorandfrancis.com
Taylor & Francis Verlag GmbH, Kaufingerstraße 24, 80331 München, Germany

9 781032 551302